ESSENTIALS
of Foreign
Exchange
Trading

ESSENTIALS SERIES

The Essentials Series was created for busy business advisory and corporate professionals. The books in this series were designed so that these busy professionals can quickly acquire knowledge and skills in core business areas.

Each book provides need-to-have fundamentals for those professionals who must:

- Get up to speed quickly, because they have been promoted to a new position or have broadened their responsibility scope
- Manage a new functional area
- Brush up on new developments in their area of responsibility
- Add more value to their company or clients

Other books in this series include:

For more information on any of the above titles, please visit www.wiley.com

ESSENTIALS
of Foreign Exchange Trading

James Chen

WILEY

John Wiley & Sons, Inc.

Copyright © 2009 by James Chen. All rights reserved.

Published by John Wiley & Sons, Inc., Hoboken, New Jersey.

Published simultaneously in Canada.

No part of this publication may be reproduced, stored in a retrieval system, or transmitted in any form or by any means, electronic, mechanical, photocopying, recording, scanning, or otherwise, except as permitted under Section 107 or 108 of the 1976 United States Copyright Act, without either the prior written permission of the Publisher, or authorization through payment of the appropriate per-copy fee to the Copyright Clearance Center, Inc., 222 Rosewood Drive, Danvers, MA 01923, 978-750-8400, fax 978-646-8600, or on the Web at www.copyright.com. Requests to the Publisher for permission should be addressed to the Permissions Department, John Wiley & Sons, Inc., 111 River Street, Hoboken, NJ 07030, 201-748-6011, fax 201-748-6008, or online at http://www.wiley.com/go/permissions.

Limit of Liability/Disclaimer of Warranty: While the publisher and author have used their best efforts in preparing this book, they make no representations or warranties with respect to the accuracy or completeness of the contents of this book and specifically disclaim any implied warranties of merchantability or fitness for a particular purpose. No warranty may be created or extended by sales representatives or written sales materials. The advice and strategies contained herein may not be suitable for your situation. You should consult with a professional where appropriate. Neither the publisher nor author shall be liable for any loss of profit or any other commercial damages, including but not limited to special, incidental, consequential, or other damages.

For general information on our other products and services, or technical support, please contact our Customer Care Department within the United States at 800-762-2974, outside the United States at 317-572-3993 or fax 317-572-4002.

Wiley also publishes its books in a variety of electronic formats. Some content that appears in print may not be available in electronic books.

For more information about Wiley products, visit our Web site at http://www.wiley.com.

Library of Congress Cataloging-in-Publication Data:

Chen, James.

    Essentials of foreign exchange trading / James Chen.

      p. cm. — (Essentials series)

    Includes index.

    ISBN 978-0-470-39086-3 (pbk.)

  1. Foreign exchange market. 2. Foreign exchange futures. 3. Investments. I. Title. II. Series.

    HG3851.C437 2009

    332.4'5—dc22

                                  2008048193

Printed in the United States of America

10 9 8 7 6 5 4 3 2

To my parents, my wife, my children, and forex traders everywhere.

Contents

Contents

Contents

Contents

Preface

Foreign exchange trading has developed at such a blinding speed within the last decade that is has garnered an unprecedented amount of interest from all corners of the globe. The meteoric rise of forex can be attributed to the many advantages of trading currencies over other financial markets. These advantages will all be discussed within the pages of this book.

More important than recognizing how forex trading can work to your benefit, however, is knowing exactly how to approach this fascinating market with the proper prudence, attitude, and methodology to achieve consistent profitability. Only in this way can the advantages of forex trading truly be realized. This book will assist you in learning many of the most important aspects of playing the currency game effectively.

I personally began my journey in forex trading when the retail foreign exchange industry was still in its early infancy. Before I ever even looked at a price chart of a currency pair or followed a forex news feed, I placed a live trade on the EUR/USD with real money. When a substantial sum was lost on that first trade, I placed another trade. And then another. And yet another. Admittedly, I kept doing this until I lost almost every single penny in my trading account. I had absolutely no rational reason or justification to place any of those first several trades in that initial trading account. To me, at that time, forex was purely a game of instinct and gut feel.

Needless to say, those early days taught me a good lesson. Most humans are not instinctively good at trading. For the vast majority of us, guts and instinct left unchecked invariably lead to catastrophic losses at some point in time, usually sooner rather than later. On attaining this realization, I began a tireless quest to become a profitable forex trader. My efforts consisted of a prolonged, single-minded endeavor to absorb forex-specific analytical methodologies, highly touted currency trading strategies, and sound money management techniques. My search for the "holy grail" of foreign exchange trading had begun in earnest.

Over time, I realized that this holy grail of forex, in the traditional sense, was not only elusive but most likely nonexistent. I came to the conclusion that although a bunch of chart indicators all flashing the same signal at the same exact time to enter into a currency trade is a very nice thing to see, it probably would not by itself be able to feed a typical family on a consistent basis. The true holy grail, I eventually found, is a combination of good analytical and trading technique, great risk/money management, and phenomenal discipline. Without these vital components, consistent profitability in forex trading would be difficult to achieve.

This is where the book you are holding comes in. It is not meant to be an exhaustive tome that covers every detailed aspect of the foreign exchange world. Rather, this book is meant to serve as a practical guide to help you develop some of the most important tools and attributes necessary for approaching forex trading in an intelligent and well-prepared manner. *Essentials of Foreign Exchange Trading* is the kind of book that I wish I had read during the earlier years of my forex trading career.

But even now, after many years of trading this market and analyzing foreign exchange price movements for countless traders around the globe on behalf of FX Solutions, I occasionally find myself neglecting some of the essential concepts of good forex trading. Therefore, I have included all of these key concepts within the pages of this book—writing them down in this manner has helped me to refocus on what is truly important in one's quest for profitability in this market.

In short, this book is highly relevant for all who strive to increase their probability of achieving success in forex trading.

Once you have read through and digested this book, I would be happy to receive any comments and/or questions you may have. Learning to trade foreign exchange is most certainly a pursuit best accomplished by interacting with other forex traders. In that spirit, you can reach me at anytime simply by e-mailing author@ fxtradingbook.com. I welcome your thoughts.

James Chen

Acknowledgments

First and foremost, I would like to give special thanks to my parents, Shou Lien and Hsiao-wen; my wife, Dongping; and my sons, Tommy and Kevin. Your tireless love, support, and encouragement both in life and throughout the entire frenzied writing process have truly been priceless.

I would also like to acknowledge my many colleagues at FX Solutions who have consistently shown tremendous interest and support during the course of my writing this book.

In addition, I would like to thank the wonderful editors at John Wiley & Sons for having demonstrated a great deal of confidence in this book project and in me as its author.

And very importantly, I would like to give a special acknowledgment to all of the forex traders around the world who have made foreign exchange trading what it is today. Without you, this book would not be possible.

CHAPTER 1

Introduction to Foreign Exchange Trading

After reading this chapter, you will be able to:

- Understand the basic facts and history of the global foreign exchange market.
- Appreciate the characteristics that set forex apart from other financial markets.
- Assess who the real market players are, and how they may affect currency prices.
- Decide whether foreign exchange trading is right for you.
- Know what to expect from this book.

Trading Money to Make Money

Foreign exchange trading is essentially about trading money. There are several reasons why people and institutions would want to trade money. The two primary reasons are currency conversion and speculation. Currency conversion is simply the changing of money from one currency to another for the primary purpose of purchasing goods, services, or assets from a foreign country. For an American company to buy British goods, for example, would necessitate the conversion of U.S. dollars to British pounds.

This book will focus exclusively on foreign exchange trading for speculative purposes, or trading money with the explicit goal of making money. This speculation process is very similar to trading in stocks or futures. The goal, whether on a long-term or short-term basis, is to earn profits from price changes. Just as a stock like Microsoft will move up and down in price, currencies will also move up and down in price. The real trick is to be on the right side of the move, and to reap profits in return for assuming the risk of taking the trade.

Of course, there are many important ways in which trading foreign exchange is completely different from trading stocks or futures, but the primary objective is the same. If a trader buys shares in Microsoft, for instance, the hope is that the value of the shares will go up and the trader will earn profits. In the same vein, if a trader buys the Japanese yen, the hope is that the value of the yen increases so that the trader will earn a profit on owning that currency.

Learning how to make money by trading money is not an easy task. There are many factors that combine to make any given foreign exchange trader a successful one. This combination usually includes plenty of often painful trading experience, good risk management skills, solid technical and fundamental analytical abilities, and a sound psychological make-up. All of these will be discussed in detail further along in the book.

To begin with, though, an introduction to the world of foreign exchange trading is in order. This will cover all of the basics, and will begin with a very brief history lesson.

Striking Gold

Although money in one form or another has been around pretty much since the beginning of time, modern speculative foreign exchange trading (also known as "FX," "forex," or "currency trading") is considered to have begun on a major scale relatively recently. In modern times, the world's currencies truly began to float freely and be traded extensively in the early 1970s, after the collapse of the Bretton Woods Agreements.

These agreements, established during the tail-end of World War II in July 1944, came about as a result of meetings between representatives of all the Allied nations in Bretton Woods, New Hampshire, U.S.A.

Among other accomplishments resulting from Bretton Woods, each of these nations agreed to adopt a monetary policy that would effectively fix the exchange rate of its currency in relation to the U.S. dollar, which in turn would be fixed to gold at a rate of USD $35.00 per ounce of gold. These changes were akin to reinstating characteristics of the Gold Standard, but this time via the U.S. dollar.

Clearly, with the Bretton Woods Agreements in place, foreign exchange trading on any significant scale was virtually impossible and nonproductive due to the nonfloating nature of currency values. While the valiant purposes of Bretton Woods were to control conflict, maintain monetary stability, and discourage currency speculation, the agreements underwent increasing pressure as the U.S. suspended the dollar's convertibility into gold in 1971. The Bretton Woods Agreements finally collapsed in the same year.

By 1973, with the complete collapse of Bretton Woods and other similar agreements that strived to impose order on the global currency system, the world's currencies truly began to float much more freely. This meant that the market forces of supply and demand would take precedence over international political consensus, and that mass speculation by banks and institutions would soon become rampant. Although most individual traders could not take part in the new market, this time period marked the birth of modern-day forex trading as we know it today.

Buying and Selling at Retail

Fast forward to around 1996, as computers and the Internet began making online financial trading both practical and in demand. With stock trading starting to go online, foreign exchange brokers/market-makers began emerging to create and satisfy a new demand for retail forex trading. Prior to this time, access to speculative forex trading was reserved almost exclusively for banks and large institutions. With the advent of online platform trading, however, access for the average individual trader/investor opened up in a major way.

This new frontier of retail currency trading was in the arena of "spot forex," which was clearly differentiated from futures and forwards. Spot foreign exchange trading is distinguished by its almost immediate delivery of the currency, rather than future delivery. Of course, in speculative currency trading, the actual physical currency never gets delivered—delivery is simply "rolled over" continuously to the next delivery date ad infinitum (or until the trading position is closed). The foreign exchange broker performs this important function in order to facilitate speculative trading, as opposed to having customers actually convert money to/from a foreign currency. In spot forex, the customary delivery settlement timeframe for most currency trades is the date of trade execution plus two days (T+2).

Big and Liquid, Like the Ocean

There are many characteristics that set the modern-day foreign exchange market apart from other financial markets like equities (stocks) and futures. Many of these characteristics help to make foreign exchange an appealing market for traders and investors coming from other financial markets.

When most people first hear about the foreign exchange market, they are usually introduced first to the sheer size of the global forex system. Along with this size comes a magnitude of liquidity almost unimaginable in any other financial market. Liquidity is defined simply as the degree to which an asset, like a currency, can be bought or sold in the market without having a significant effect on the asset's price. The liquidity of currencies, especially the "major" ones like the U.S. dollar and the euro, is unrivaled by any other financial instrument, including stocks, bonds, and futures contracts.

Among other implications of this high level of liquidity, because of the staggeringly high volume of transactions and the countless number of traders (both institutional and retail) involved in this market, it is extremely difficult for any individual market participant to manipulate foreign exchange prices artificially in any significant manner.

This blanket statement, however, notably excludes the world's central banks (e.g., the U.S. Federal Reserve (the Fed), the European Central Bank (ECB), the Bank of Japan (BOJ)), which can and do attempt to manipulate the markets. This type of manipulation activity, however, has become an accepted part of the forex trading game, and generally does not offer an unfair advantage to any speculative market participant. Furthermore, central bank attempts to manipulate currencies for the purposes of furthering national economic policy are usually much easier to accept than, for example, the profit-minded manipulation of individual stocks by often unscrupulous traders.

Apart from potential central bank manipulation, just how big is the foreign exchange market that it can claim its place as the most liquid market the world has known? According to the most recent statistics issued by the Bank for International Settlements (BIS), which serves as an international organization and "bank for central banks," the average daily turnover in the primary foreign exchange markets is estimated to be around $3.2 trillion (as of April 2007). This figure represents an unprecedented three-year growth rate of 69%, and far eclipses the volume traded in any other financial market in the world.

Of this $3.2 trillion, about $1 trillion is in "spot" foreign exchange trades, which, as mentioned earlier, are forex trades that are distinguished by immediate delivery of the currency. Spot foreign exchange is the type of trading that most individual traders in the retail forex market are primarily concerned with. While some individual traders get involved with currency futures and other derivative financial instruments, the growth of the spot foreign exchange arena has largely eclipsed these smaller markets.

Open 24/5

Besides the sheer size and liquidity of the foreign exchange markets, which can certainly be a great advantage to the average speculative trader, another distinguishing characteristic of forex is its global, decentralized nature. Essentially, it is an over-the-counter (OTC) market, where the different currency trading locations around the globe electronically form a unified, interconnected market entity. Among other advantages stemming from this fact, all currencies can be traded electronically 24 hours a day as the major global markets open, overlap, and close, one after another.

From the perspective of New York time (U.S. Eastern Time), the markets open up as follows.

The very beginning of the week falls on Sunday afternoon in New York, when the New Zealand banks open at 2:00 PM New York time. At 5:00 PM (still New York time) the financial markets in Sydney, Australia, open. Tokyo then opens at 7:00 PM, followed by Hong Kong and Singapore concurrently at 9:00 PM. At this point, all five of these currency-trading financial markets are open: New Zealand, Australia; Japan; Hong Kong; and Singapore.

In the wee hours of Monday, Frankfurt, Germany, opens up the primary euro market at 2:00 AM, New York time. By this time,

New Zealand and Australia are already closed, and the East Asian markets of Tokyo, Hong Kong, and Singapore are on their last legs. The European time zone continues shortly thereafter with the opening of the pivotal London session. Customarily the market with the most liquidity (as most foreign exchange trading has traditionally occurred within the London market), London session opens an hour after Frankfurt, at 3:00 AM NY time.

Finally, at 8:00 AM on Monday morning, the New York financial markets are the last of the major global markets to open. Since New York is also a strong foreign exchange trading market, much like London and Frankfurt, the overlap between these three markets— around 8:00 to 11:00 AM NY time—represents among the most active, liquid, and volatile trading hours available in forex. At the same time, however, the period surrounding the London opening currently takes the crown for the most active foreign exchange market.

A couple of hours before the close of the New York market, the New Zealand market opens up again at 2:00 PM to begin the whole globe-hopping process all over again. After Monday, this seamless process continues on every weekday until Friday, when the close of the last foreign exchange market in New York signals the end of the trading week at around 4:00 to 5:00 PM New York time. Therefore, from around 2:00 PM on Sunday to 5:00 PM on Friday, forex trading takes place 24 hours a day, five days a week.

One important note to keep in mind about trading currencies at all hours of the day and night is that even though a particular market happens to be closed, it does not mean that the currency specific to that market is not being traded. For example, when London opens in the middle of the night in New York while the U.S. markets are closed, some of the most active trading of the U.S. dollar occurs. Beginning traders are often under the mistaken impression that a country's currency is only traded when that country's markets happen to be open. This is untrue only because the foreign exchange markets are traded by people and institutions around the world via a global, decentralized network. Therefore, U.S. dollar trading, for example, is not dependent on the business hours of any centralized, physical exchange located in the United States.

The fact that foreign exchange can be traded 24 hours a day means that traders have the advantage of choosing when it is most convenient to trade, considering their own personal schedules. For this reason, many traders hold full-time jobs while trading forex during off-hours. This provides a tremendous amount of flexibility that is not offered in other major trading markets. Of course, those traders that choose to take advantage of the most active markets must necessarily watch the currencies during the most active times, like during London or New York market openings. But the fact that all currencies can be traded 24 hours a day means that there is almost always price movement available upon which to trade.

Playing in the Majors

Just because there is price movement in a given currency does not necessarily mean that the currency is liquid and heavily traded. On the contrary; although the number of currencies in regular use around the world comes close to the number of countries in existence, only a very small handful of these currencies make up the vast majority of forex trading volume. This is yet another unique characteristic of the foreign exchange market in comparison to other financial markets, and it can certainly be considered an advantage for traders.

According to the BIS, the most-traded currency, by far, is the U.S. dollar, with consistently greater than 85% of the average daily turnover in foreign exchange trading. The distant second place currency is the Eurozone's euro, with around a 37% share. Rounding out the top currencies are the Japanese yen with approximately 16%, and the British pound with 15% (because there are two currencies in each traded pair, the percentages of all the currencies combined, including the top-traded currencies cited above, will equal 200% instead of 100%.). The structure of currency pairs as they are traded in the foreign exchange market will be discussed in Chapter 2, which covers basic trading mechanics.

Because of the fact that only a few currencies form most of the activity in the foreign exchange market, which means that these currencies are the most liquid and active, it is usually recommended for beginning traders to concentrate initially just on the major currencies. This avoids confusion and promotes focus in trading.

When matched together into predetermined currency pairings (as will be described further in Chapter 2), these currencies make up the four "majors." These majors are all U.S. dollar-based and include, first and foremost, the EUR/USD (euro against U.S. dollar). This key currency pair is considered not only the most actively traded currency pair available, but also the most actively traded financial instrument in the world.

Following behind EUR/USD are USD/JPY (U.S. dollar against Japanese yen), and GBP/USD (British pound against U.S. dollar).

Finally, USD/CHF (U.S. dollar against Swiss franc) has even less liquidity because of the progressively diminishing market activity of the Swiss franc over the years, but it is still considered one of the majors. AUD/USD (Australian dollar against U.S. dollar) and USD/CAD (U.S. dollar against Canadian dollar) are next in line in terms of trading activity, but are not generally considered among the majors.

IN THE REAL WORLD

Currency Terminology

As in other businesses and industries, foreign exchange trading has evolved its own vernacular over time. To outsiders, some of the terminology used by professional forex traders may seem a bit peculiar. But it has become virtually a language unto itself for those that deal with currencies on a daily basis. Here are some of the most common examples of currency terminology:

Currency or Currency Pair	Common Terminology
GBP (British Pound)	Sterling
CAD (Canadian Dollar)	Loonie
USD (U.S. Dollar)	Greenback
AUD (Australian Dollar)	Aussie
NZD (New Zealand Dollar)	Kiwi
EUR/USD (Euro/U.S. Dollar)	Euro
GBP/USD (British Pound/U.S. Dollar)	Cable
USD/JPY (U.S. Dollar/Japanese Yen)	Dollar-Yen
USD/CHF (U.S. Dollar/Swiss Franc)	Dollar-Swiss or Swissy
USD/CAD (U.S. Dollar/Canadian Dollar)	Dollar-Canada

Unlike stock trading, where there are countless possible securities to choose from, foreign exchange trading is much simpler and more straightforward in terms of selecting trades. Sticking to the majors—as many foreign exchange participants are wisely apt to do—allows traders to focus their efforts in an efficient manner rather than disperse their attention among a multitude of different securities. In a time marked by progressively increasing information overload, a limited set of trading options can certainly be seen as a significant benefit.

Leveraged to the Hilt

Another feature of foreign exchange trading that differentiates it from other financial markets is the astronomical levels of leverage that are commonplace in the forex world. The specifics of utilizing this leverage will be discussed in Chapter 2. For now, though, it should be known that many foreign exchange brokers will offer up to 400:1 leverage on the average retail trading account. This means that $1 in a trader's forex account can control up to $400 in a currency trade. The implications of this are mind-boggling. No other major financial market offers even close to this kind of leverage.

As will be discussed further in Chapter 2, however, this can be both a very positive feature as well as a very negative one. By definition, leverage is a type of financial magnification. While it is true that high leverage magnifies profits, it will also magnify losses equally. Oftentimes, it is this high level of leverage that summarily wipes out otherwise healthy trading accounts. Used with a great deal of caution, however, high leverage of the magnitude found in forex trading can offer tremendous possibilities to the upside as well as to the downside.

The Players

Knowing and understanding who the primary players are within the foreign exchange market goes a long way in helping individual traders approach the market in an informed manner. In terms of market impact, the most influential group of participants in the forex market would have to be the major banks. From the perspective of speculative trading, these banks have a great deal of funds to throw around, and the traders at many of these banks are responsible for moving astronomical amounts of money. Of course, banks also do a lot of nonspeculative currency exchanges for clients, but the speculative activity is really what moves the currency markets in the most dramatic manner. When there are big, sudden moves in currency prices, more often than not the banks, as a collective entity, are behind a good portion of the move.

Next in the hierarchy of speculative currency traders would have to be the hedge funds and other investment firms. In recent years, these entities, which often control a great deal of discretionary client equity, have progressively increased their speculative activities in foreign exchange. Because of the sheer enormity of the funds at their disposal, some of these firms come close to rivaling the major banks in their power to influence the currency markets.

Other participants in the foreign exchange market are not generally considered speculative players, and therefore may not be as influential in their trading activities as the participants described above. These include the central banks, which, as discussed earlier, are not considered speculative in their market activities. Rather, central banks get in the game primarily to further their economic policy agendas.

Because of their vast importance in helping ultimately to determine currency value, however, central banks certainly have the potential to impact currency prices with their attempts at currency manipulation.

Companies wishing to convert their funds to a foreign currency in order to purchase foreign goods or services are another example of nonspeculative market players. When their currency exchange activities are factored in collectively, these companies may help partially determine the course of international trade flow. Though this collective activity can certainly have some lasting impact on the currency markets, it is perhaps not influential enough to be of great significance to speculative foreign exchange traders.

The last group of market participants in foreign exchange is, by far, the smallest and least significant with regard to influence on the market as a whole. This group consists most notably of people like you, the individual retail trader. Whether you have $100 or $100,000 or even more to trade through your retail forex broker, none of your trading activity will likely ever move the currency markets in any appreciable way. That is not to say that you are at all unimportant. Rather, it just means that your trades, along with those of every other individual forex trader combined, will probably never influence the direction of the vast foreign exchange market. This, again, goes back to the sheer size and liquidity of the market, as well as the fact that its activity is so overwhelmingly dominated by well-heeled financial institutions whose funds dwarf those of individual retail traders.

But while retail traders, via their brokers, will unlikely ever influence the course of the foreign exchange market, they can certainly learn how to trade it effectively and hopefully to extract profit from it. That is precisely the goal for the rest of this book. From basic forex trading mechanics to common analytical methods to specific trading strategies and risk management techniques, this book is intended to steer individual traders effectively through the maze that is foreign exchange trading.

What Moves the Forex Markets?

In order to steer through this maze successfully, foreign exchange traders should become familiar with the forces that drive this market. Although there are many traders who insist that market drivers, or causes of price fluctuations, are unimportant because everything is already reflected in price action on the charts, it would be a grave mistake to ignore the fundamental roots of market movement. As will be discussed further in Chapter 4 on fundamental analysis, knowing what moves the forex market is integral to becoming an informed, and therefore well-equipped, foreign exchange trader.

The primary movers of currency exchange rates are all tied to the basic forces of economics, as will be described in detail within Chapter 4. For now, though, a simplification of the cause of currency exchange rate movement can be said to relate directly to the process of international capital flow. This is simply the movement of money from one currency to another. International capital flows, in turn, are caused by basic economic supply and demand factors.

As will be expounded on in Chapter 4, supply and demand are determined by a number of different factors. Most notably, these factors include a country's interest rates, inflation situation, GDP growth, employment, trade balance, and other barometers of economic health. If demand for a currency increases (and/or supply decreases) as a result of one or a combination of these factors, that currency's exchange rate will generally increase in relation to other currencies. Conversely, if demand for a currency decreases (and/or supply increases) as a result of one or a combination of the factors above, that currency's exchange rate will generally decrease in relation to other currencies. It is a simple concept, but one that is not so simple to utilize in attempting to forecast market directions.

Aside from the fundamental market drivers just described, technical factors are often overlooked or underestimated in their ability to help move the forex markets. Although this will all be discussed in great detail in Chapter 3, a brief explanation here will help illustrate the point.

Traders in many banks, hedge funds, and other potential market-moving institutions will often use certain techniques of technical analysis to help them make trading decisions. These traders all have access to the same price charts. Furthermore, these charts all show the same patterns, key price levels, and technical phenomena, with perhaps just some minor differences due to variations in the traders' individual interpretations.

This means that these influential players are generally all seeing the same types of technical events on the charts, which will often prompt many of them to buy at a similar price level, as well as sell at a similar price level. When a great deal of institutional money is on the same side of the market at the same approximate price level, prices can and will be influenced in one direction or another. In fact, this phenomenon of collective trading activity by influential market players is considered one of the primary causes of support and resistance levels being respected so precisely in many instances. One of the most significant concepts in foreign exchange trading, support/resistance will be explored in much more detail in Chapter 3, which covers technical analysis.

What to Expect from This Book

The core of this book begins with in-depth descriptions of basic foreign exchange trading mechanics in Chapter 2. This includes all of the terminology and explanations necessary to get started in foreign exchange trading. From the structure of a currency pair to the intricacies of margin and leverage as they pertain to forex trading, Chapter 2 will get true beginners up and running quickly. The chapter is also directed at experienced traders coming from other financial markets, serving as a thorough discourse on the unique intricacies of trading currencies.

Following the chapter on basic trading mechanics is Chapter 3, which is a comprehensive discussion of technical analysis as it is applied to foreign exchange trading. The tools of technical analysis are perhaps the most tangible and accessible trading tools available to the individual foreign exchange trader. Software programs used specifically for charting prices in the foreign exchange market abound, and they provide the most popular way for most currency traders to make trading decisions. From free-hand trendlines to mathematically derived chart indicators to complex pattern formations, the primary tools of technical analysis, as they are used to trade forex market movement, will be the sole focus of Chapter 3.

Next is Chapter 4, which is devoted exclusively to fundamental analysis as it applies to foreign exchange trading. This important discipline can best be described as the study of factors that drive currency exchange rate movement. From interest rates to inflation to economic growth and much more, the fundamental concepts described in Chapter 4 provide an essential foundation of knowledge for forex traders who wish to understand what really makes the foreign exchange markets tick.

Moving on to Chapter 5, this is where the knowledge gained in previous chapters can be put to practical use. Chapter 5 is all about foreign exchange trading methods and strategies, or the ways in which top currency traders tackle the markets on a daily basis. Included in this chapter are sections on strategic trading based on trends, breakouts, chart patterns, news, interest carry, divergences, multiple timeframes, and much more. The methods and strategies contained in this chapter provide traders with practical ideas that can be used almost immediately to trade forex.

Finally, Chapter 6 closes the book with some extremely important elements of trading. This chapter is found at the end of the book because it introduces perhaps the most advanced concepts in the book, and not because its contents are any less important than other subjects. On the contrary, concepts like risk and money management, trading discipline, and the optimal trader's psychology, are often considered by experienced traders to be among the most important components of a successful trading career. Since many beginning traders instead believe that finding the best trade entry point is the most crucial aspect of good trading, it is especially imperative that these novice traders pay particularly close attention to Chapter 6.

As a whole, this book should serve as a solid introduction and guide to the fascinating world of foreign exchange trading. Much more can be said about the minute intricacies of how this market works. But in order to learn how it really works, the very best teacher beyond this book on the essentials is a lot of hands-on experience. Nothing beats getting your hands dirty by getting in there and actually practicing. Fortunately, this is extremely easy in today's retail currency trading environment. Virtually every reputable forex broker offers free practice account demos of their trading platforms, complete with real-time prices, charting software, and newsfeed services. With these convenient resources at every prospective forex trader's fingertips, there is absolutely no excuse not to get out there and start trading currencies with play money in a practice account.

Chapter Summary

In this introduction to *Essentials of Foreign Exchange Trading*, a brief history and description of the development of the foreign exchange market was touched upon. After the collapse of the Bretton Woods Agreements, which essentially fixed exchange rates, speculative currency trading was able to develop in an extremely rapid manner.

Fast forward to the past decade or so, and this development became even more rapid with the help of the Internet and technology enhancements. Modern-day spot forex trading via retail electronic platforms has opened up new opportunities for legions of individual traders.

Characteristics inherent in the foreign exchange market that differentiate it from other financial markets include the fact that it is the most heavily traded market in the world, by far. This ensures that its liquidity is second to none. Another differentiating characteristic is that forex is open 24 hours a day (except weekends), as the market travels seamlessly around the globe with the changing time zones. Other notable distinguishing features include the fact that there are only a handful of tradable currencies to worry about, as opposed to countless stocks and options, as well as the fact that forex offers extremely high leverage levels (currently up to 400:1).

The key speculative players in the foreign exchange market include the major commercial and investment banks, as well as the larger hedge funds. The lowest rung on the totem pole of influential participants consists of individual retail traders. Although there may be a great deal of enthusiasm in this group, individual traders are generally unable to move the forex markets in any appreciable way.

The primary drivers of foreign exchange price movement include key fundamental factors like interest rates, GDP, employment, and inflation, which all help affect the basic economic supply and demand situation for each currency. Besides the fundamentals, technical factors can also contribute significantly to exchange rate movement.

Finally, the rest of the chapters in this book were introduced. In its entirety, this book serves as an essential guide to foreign exchange trading, as the title suggests. But nothing could ever take the place of hands-on, practical experience. Forex traders are fortunate to have their pick of free demo practice accounts provided by forex brokers. These accounts generally differ from real accounts only by the kind of money traded (play money versus real money). Therefore, it is incumbent upon the serious student of forex to practice diligently with these demo accounts, as no better method exists of gaining invaluable experience and self-directed education at no cost.

CHAPTER 2

Basic Foreign Exchange Trading Mechanics

After reading this chapter, you will be able to:

- Appreciate the unique structure of currency pairs.
- Place foreign exchange trades using any type of trade order.
- Understand the mechanics behind stop losses and profit limits.
- Recognize how lot size, leverage, and margin can affect your trading.
- Identify the potential transaction costs involved in forex trading, including spreads and interest.

Anatomy of a Currency Pair

The foreign exchange market is traded in a very unique way when compared with other major financial markets like stocks or futures. Unlike these more traditional markets, foreign exchange trading is accomplished using the relative value of the underlying instrument, rather than the absolute value.

More specifically, currencies are traded in pairs. When forex traders talk about trading the U.S. dollar, for example, they are really talking about trading the U.S. dollar's relative value against another currency. This other currency could be the euro, the British pound, the Japanese yen, or even the Thai baht, among many others. The first currency in a currency pair is called the "base" currency, while the second currency is called the "quote" (or "counter") currency.

It cannot be emphasized enough how important it is to keep in mind that there are two integral, opposing components of a traded currency pair, instead of the single component prevalent in trading stocks or futures. When forex traders initiate market positions, it is imperative that they take into consideration the relative value of both currencies. This means that a trader should not just consider whether a currency will go up or down in value. Rather, the trader must always take into account whether the currency's value will go up or down in comparison with another currency.

For example, one of the most commonly traded currency pairs is the USD/JPY, which can be described in longhand as the U.S. dollar against the Japanese yen. If traders maintain the view that the value of the U.S. dollar will rise in relation to the Japanese yen, they will buy the USD/JPY pair. Conversely, if they think that the

U.S. dollar will fall in relation to the Japanese yen, they will sell the USD/JPY pair.

Logically, by the same token, if traders believe that the yen will rise in relation to the dollar, they will sell USD/JPY. And if they think the yen will fall against the dollar, they will buy USD/JPY. At first this may appear confusing. But if one considers currency pairs as a coupling of polar opposites, it becomes a lot easier to grasp with some time and experience.

As a point of reference, the top tier of currency pairs are the four "majors," which consist of the most traded, and therefore most liquid, U.S. dollar-based pairs. These are EUR/USD (euro against U.S. dollar), USD/JPY (U.S. dollar against Japanese yen), GBP/USD (British pound against U.S. dollar), and USD/CHF (U.S. dollar against Swiss franc).

Then, there are the "semi-major" pairs, which also contain the U.S. dollar but are not traded as actively as the majors. These include USD/CAD (U.S. dollar against Canadian dollar) and AUD/USD (Australian dollar against U.S. dollar).

After these, there are the many significant "crosses" which, by definition, do not contain the U.S. dollar. Crosses include EUR/GBP (euro against British pound), AUD/NZD (Australian dollar against New Zealand dollar), CAD/JPY (Canadian dollar against Japanese yen), GBP/CHF (British pound against Swiss franc), and EUR/JPY (euro against Japanese yen), among others.

And finally, the exotics, which are thinly traded on the global forex market compared to the more popular majors and crosses, round out the currency pair list. These pairs include such currencies as the Hungarian forint (HUF), the Malaysian ringgit (MYR), and the South African rand (ZAR), among numerous others.

Going Long and Selling Short

The fact that currencies are traded in pairs differentiates the foreign exchange market from other financial markets in important ways, one of which is the concept of long and short.

In trading equities, for example, a "long" entry is simply the process of buying shares in a specific security in the hope that it will go up in value. Conversely, a "short" entry is to sell shares before actually owning them. This is with the understanding that the shares must be bought back or "covered" at a later date, hopefully for a profit if the stock goes down. Consequently, if traders believe that a stock will go up, they will enter the trade "long." If, on the other hand, they think it will go down in price, they will sell "short."

The foreign exchange market, in contrast, treats long and short in a significantly different manner. To be long EUR/USD, for example, is to simultaneously buy euro and sell dollar. To be short EUR/USD, on the other hand, is to simultaneously sell euro and buy dollar. So whether one is long or short any given currency pair, one is always long one of the currencies in the pair, and short the other.

This concept may seem foreign to traders used to dealing with stocks and/or futures, but it essentially means that no matter what position a trader takes in the currency markets, that trader is always both bullish (financially optimistic) on one currency while simultaneously bearish (financially pessimistic) on another.

Now that the structure of currency pairs has been established, the all-important topics of order type and trade placement can be discussed.

Robert R. Prechter Jr.

Robert R. Prechter Jr., CMT, famed publisher of *The Elliott Wave Theorist* since 1979, is founder/president of Elliott Wave International (elliottwave.com) and executive director of the Socionomics Institute. Legendary for his market timing and trading acumen utilizing Elliott Wave principles, Prechter has won numerous major accolades from the media and financial community over an illustrious, decades-long career. He has authored many books, several of which were instrumental in bringing Ralph Nelson Elliott's groundbreaking Elliott Wave Principle into the forefront of financial market analysis.

Prechter states:

"Currencies help us understand a fundamental aspect of markets. They make clear that all markets are simply ratios."

"Stock indexes are expressions of share values in terms of some currency. For example, the Dow Jones Industrial Average is the ratio of an average of 30 Dow stocks relative to dollars. But one could just as well express the ratio as its inverse, showing the value of a dollar in terms of 30 Dow stocks. Then, instead of watching the Dow go up and down, investors would be watching the dollar go up and down in terms of a certain group of 30 stocks. They would be talking about how their dollars are doing instead of how their stocks are doing."

"Many people have difficulty understanding the simple fact that markets are ratios. Thankfully, currency markets illustrate the matter clearly. A U.S. investor can observe the dollar going up and down by watching the dollar/euro ratio. A European can watch the euro go up and down by watching the euro/dollar ratio. Each of these two investors—if he hasn't thought about the matter—might have a different psychological orientation to his local expression of the ratio. But that doesn't change the fact—obvious in this instance—that both investors are looking at exactly the same information. 'Up' and 'down' have no real referent."

"Most stock investors are married to the idea that up is good and down is bad. There is some basis for truth in this feeling, because a downtrend in the stock market indicates a trend toward more negative social mood, which in turn has negative results in social action. But in terms of investment success, the direction is irrelevant, and feelings of 'good' and 'bad' only get in the way of successful decision-making."

"A currency investor has an advantage over a stock investor, because he should be far less married to feelings of whether a certain direction for a ratio is 'good' or 'bad.' In the currency trader's world, there is no qualitative difference between the numerator and the denominator. On one side of the ratio is one currency, and on the other side is another. There is not even properly an 'up' or a 'down' direction. Every move is both directions, depending on how you express the ratio. The point is that a currency investor should be able to approach his craft with less psychological baggage than a stock investor carries and therefore with more objectivity and a better chance of success. This difference makes it easier for a currency analyst to see that his job is not to 'hope' or 'fear' but just to get the trends right. If all investors could learn that lesson, they would be better off."

Market Orders—On the Spot

Depending on the specific strategy or type of trading preferred, foreign exchange traders often rely heavily upon market orders. A market order simply means that a trader wishes to enter a currency position at the present moment, whether it is an order to buy (long) or sell (short) a specific currency pair.

The main functionality that differentiates this type of order from others is the fact that a market order is executed at the current market price, as opposed to a future price level.

Market orders are primarily used by traders who are physically at their trading stations watching the market, waiting for either a specific technical chart setup or a fundamental news announcement. Once one of these trading opportunities presents itself, the trader is then able to establish a virtually instant market position through the use of a well-placed market order.

Entry Orders—Waiting until the Price Is Right

In contrast to the immediate nature of market orders, entry orders are pending positions whose purpose is to trigger when a certain price level is reached. These types of orders can be set to execute well ahead of time, and will only be executed if the specified price is reached.

There are two primary types of entry orders—stop entries and limit entries. In the retail foreign exchange market, the functional discrepancy between these two entry order types is largely semantic, and many brokers simply blur the differences by calling them both limit orders. But for those forex brokers that keep the delineation intact, traders simply need to learn and remember the definitions, which are as follows:

Buy stop—an entry order to buy at a price above the current price.

Buy limit—an entry order to buy at a price below the current price.

Sell stop—an entry order to sell at a price below the current price.

Sell limit—an entry order to sell at a price above the current price.

Unlike market orders, entry orders are primarily used by traders who are unable or unwilling to be watching real-time prices and waiting for trade opportunities at their trading stations. With entry orders, complete orders can be entered ahead of time that encompass the full trading lifecycle, including both the trade entry as well as the stop loss and profit target exits. These trade exits will be discussed in more detail in the next section.

Entry orders may also be used as a tool for enforcing order entry discipline. Traders placing market orders at the current price are often prone to entering orders "on the fly," as a result of counterproductive emotions like greed and fear. In contrast, the mechanism of entry orders encourages traders to enter trades only if their specific, predetermined price level and entry rules are met. Discipline is a tremendously vital factor in successful trading that will be discussed further in Chapter 6.

Stopping Losses with Stop Losses and Trailing Stops

Whereas market orders and entry orders are trade entries, stop losses, trailing stops, and profit limits (described in the next section) are trade exits. While many beginning traders concentrate almost exclusively on entries, most intermediate and advanced traders eventually come to realize that exits are at least as important, and some say even more important, than getting the entries right.

In this section, only the basic mechanics of stop losses and trailing stops will be touched upon. Later, in Chapter 6, in a section that covers risk management, the full meaning and nuances of using stop losses will be discussed.

Stop losses are exactly what they appear to be. They actually "stop losses." A stop loss is a form of pending order that can be attached to any open order or position, whether that trade was originally a market order or an entry order.

A stop loss closes an open trade when that trade reaches a predetermined level of loss. It is the price point at which a trader no longer wishes to be involved in the trade because of the desire to limit losses to a manageable level.

When using technical analysis (which will be discussed in great detail in Chapter 3), a trader will employ a stop loss to get out of a losing trade once that trade no longer makes sense from a technical price perspective.

For example, if a currency pair's price breaks out above a critical resistance line, and a technical trader then buys the pair in hopes of profiting on a continued price climb, a sensible location for a technical stop loss would be right below the line from where price broke out. This is because if price subsequently retreats back below the line, it is no longer considered a valid breakout trade and the trade no longer makes sense. Stop losses are an incredibly useful tool for predetermining trade risk and limiting catastrophic trading losses.

The close cousin to the simple stop loss is the trailing stop loss. Whereas a stop loss is, by definition, a static order to close a trade at a predetermined loss level, a trailing stop loss is a dynamic order to close a trade at progressively better prices. The primary purpose of a trailing stop loss order is to limit losses while automatically locking in gains. A trailing stop loss accomplishes this by systematically moving the stop loss as the price moves in favor of the position.

For example, a trader buys the EUR/USD pair. The trader then wishes not only to limit losses if price goes against this long position, but also to lock-in gains if price favors the position. To accomplish this, the trader would set-up a trailing stop loss. If the stop-loss is set to trail the market price by 20 pips (the concept of pips will be described shortly), it will actually follow the price dynamically by an increment of 20 pips as the market moves, but only if the market moves in a favorable direction.

The key concept to remember is that the trailing stop will only move one way—in favor of the trader's position. If price moves against the trader's position, the trailing stop will not move. And if price moves against the trader's position by more than the predetermined trailing stop increment, the trade will automatically be closed by the trailing stop. If this occurs after a long price run in favor of the trader's position, substantial profits will have been gained while having dynamically limited losses from the outset.

Trailing stop losses are often key components of professional risk management strategies, and can be used to great advantage by the typical foreign exchange trader.

Profit Limits—When You're in the Money

Another important type of exit order is the profit limit. Profit limits can be considered the direct opposite of stop losses. The purpose of a profit limit order is to close an open trade automatically at a pre-determined, profitable price level so that the trader may realize those profits into the trading account.

A profit limit order is set up much like a trader would set up a stop loss order, only in the opposite direction.

Profit limits are set primarily with the intention of realizing and securing profits before price reverses and erases those profits. When foreign exchange traders set entry orders, they will often also set both stop losses and profit limits so that there is a contingency for any direction price may take within a given trade.

Exit with Caution

The last type of trade exit to be discussed here is the manual exit, or manual close. This consists of simply closing an open trade at the current market price, much like a trader would open a trade at the current market price with a market order.

Relying on manual exits instead of preset exits can be a danger-ous practice for beginners. Much like traders who overrely on mar-ket orders may be prone to opening positions haphazardly because of emotions like greed or fear, traders using manual exits may fall into the same type of trap.

Mental stops—which means a trader has an "intention" to man-ually close out a losing trade at some point of financial pain, but does not actually set the stop loss—fall into the category of manual exits. For obvious reasons, mental stops can potentially be dangerous, especially if the trader does not actually have the necessary discipline to close the losing trade and avoid a catastrophic loss.

On the profit end of the spectrum, manual exits can also be potentially disadvantageous. If a strict profit limit that conforms to a properly planned risk:reward ratio is not set (risk:reward is discussed further in Chapter 6, which covers risk management), traders are often tempted prematurely to close winning positions manually. In other words, with manual exits, fearful beginners will often close their trades too early and with too small a profit to become consistently successful traders.

Trade Size—Lots and Lots of Lots

Whether entering or exiting a currency trade, how much of a given currency is actually being bought or sold? The answer lies in the lot. The closest equivalent to a lot in the financial markets is the contract, which is standard futures trading terminology. Lots, much like the role of contracts in the futures markets, are the standardized units of trade that are bought and sold in the foreign exchange market.

There are several types of lots available to trade that are classified according to size. Standard, mini, and micro (or super-mini) are generally the main terms used by retail forex brokers and traders to describe the different tradable lot sizes. A standard lot is sized at 100,000 currency units, while a mini lot is 10,000 units, and a micro lot is 1,000 units.

These lot sizes are defined in generic unit terms because the specific currency represented by the units depends on which currency pair is traded. For example, if a standard lot of EUR/USD is traded, it would be 100,000 euros. In contrast, if it was a standard lot of AUD/JPY, the lot size would be 100,000 Australian dollars.

It is vitally important that a trader chooses a lot size that is appropriate to that trader's account size and risk tolerance. The lot size chosen by the trader affects virtually all other aspects of trading. This includes the margin required to enter and keep open a given trade; the monetary value per pip movement in price; the amount paid in spread costs; and the amount of interest paid or received. All of these topics will be described next within this chapter.

Leveraging Margin and Leverage

The concepts of margin and leverage are extremely important. Margin is the actual amount of trading equity in a trader's account that is available to use for controlling currency positions. Leverage is the multiplier by which a trader can magnify the financial controlling power of margin.

Because of the high leverage common in foreign exchange trading, a trader is able to trade a large lot amount like $100,000 with only a small fraction of this amount in trading account margin.

Common leverage ratios currently offered by foreign exchange brokers range from 50:1 on the low side all the way up to 400:1 on the high side. The sheer magnitude of this level of leverage, even on the low side, far eclipses the amount of leverage available in other financial trading markets.

In practical terms, what this means to the foreign exchange trader is that a standard lot of $100,000, for example, can be traded in the USD/CHF currency pair with only $250 in trading account margin. This is assuming that the maximum leverage of 400:1 is utilized. In other words, for every $1 that a trader has invested in a forex account, that trader can control a whopping $400 in a currency trade. In this particular example, the $250 in the trader's trading account can control a trade of $100,000, using 400:1 leverage.

Of course, like many good things in life, the massive amount of leverage offered in foreign exchange trading can be viewed as the proverbial double-edged sword. The fact that a small amount of money controls a large amount of money in forex trading can certainly serve to magnify profit potential. But on the flip side of the coin, the amount of risk inherent in highly leveraged trading like this is equally magnified.

Therefore, it is advisable to use caution when trading with the substantial leverage common in forex trading. Highly leveraged trading is aggressive trading that is characterized by both high risk and high potential reward.

Margin Call—Insufficient Funds

The risk that is assumed when trading aggressively in currencies is primarily confined to the dreaded margin call. But contrary to the popular opinion that a margin call represents the worst-case scenario for a trader, this is far from the truth. The worst case could be far worse.

A margin call is actually a safeguard to protect the trader from losing 100%, or even more, of the money in a trading account.

To owe additional funds to a broker is actually the worst-case scenario, and this uncomfortable situation is largely avoidable because of the existence of the margin call.

Unlike in the world of traditional stock trading, a margin call in foreign exchange trading is not actually a physical call from the broker to add additional funds to the margin account when equity is running low. In forex, if a trader no longer has enough equity in the trading account to keep the open position(s) viable, the trading platform software automatically closes out all open positions and immediately realizes all losses at the prevailing market rates.

Although this may seem a bit cold-hearted, there are good reasons for automated margin calls in foreign exchange trading. Prices can move extremely fast in the forex market, and because of the high leverage involved, every price move is magnified. Therefore, when a trader's equity runs low, the account can become depleted quickly and there is usually not enough time to call for more funds. As a safeguard measure, the forex margin call closes all open positions to help ensure that the trader does not lose the entire account, or worse.

So when exactly is a margin call triggered? This depends entirely on the number and size of the lot(s) traded, the leverage chosen, and the equity in the account. But generally speaking, a margin call is triggered when a trading account no longer has sufficient equity available to maintain the required margin for the positions that are currently open.

For example, suppose a trader has $2500 in a trading account, and leverage of 100:1 with a standard lot size of 100,000 units per trade have been chosen as the settings for this account. If this trader wishes to buy one lot (or GBP£100,000) of the GBP/USD pair, USD$1970 in margin is required to be put up, as per the exchange rate at the time of this writing. This is because £1000 is needed to control £100,000 at 100:1 leverage. But since the trading account is denominated in U.S. dollars, this £1000 needs to be converted into the U.S. dollar equivalent (which, at the current exchange rate, comes out to around $1970).

Each minimum price movement, or pip (explained in the next section), is worth exactly USD$10 in this scenario. If we assume that this trader does not place any stop losses and the market goes against the position, every price movement against the position will bring down the account equity by $10. So, once again, if the trader has an initial $2500 in a trading account and the margin required to keep the trade open is $1970, the account will experience a margin call and the position will automatically be closed once equity dips below $1970, which is $530 below the initial account equity. At $10 per pip, this constitutes a potential pip loss of around 53 pips (minus the spread) before margin call is reached.

The obvious problem with the example just given is that the trader entered into an inordinately large trade for the amount of funds in the trading account, and the trader also failed to use a stop loss. Of course, margin calls and even more horrible doomsday scenarios can easily be avoided just by using some good old-fashioned trading prudence. This includes using stop losses and only entering trades that are sized appropriately in proportion to the size of the trading account. This will be discussed further in the section covering risk and money management in Chapter 6.

Pips—The Currency of Currency Trading

Up to this point, pips have been lightly touched upon but not properly defined. An extremely important concept in foreign exchange trading, a pip is simply the smallest unit of price movement in the exchange rate of a currency pair. Pip can stand for "percentage in point" or "price interest point." But regardless of the exact acronym definition, its practical meaning is clear. Traders trade foreign exchange in order to earn pips. Earned pips are the reward for a good trade, while lost pips are the punishment for a bad trade.

Loosely akin to the "tick" found in other financial markets, a pip most often refers to the smallest change in the fourth decimal place of most major currencies. This would be the equivalent of 1/100th of one percent, or one basis point. The notable exception to this would be currency pairs denominated in Japanese yen, or JPY, in which a pip would constitute the smallest change in the second decimal place.

So, for the vast majority of currency pairs like EUR/USD or GBP/CHF or AUD/NZD, the exchange rate format would look like x.xxxx, where a change of 0.0001 would constitute a pip movement. On the other hand, for the handful of currency pairs featuring the yen, like USD/JPY or GBP/JPY, the exchange rate format would look like xxx.xx, where a change of 000.01 would constitute a pip movement.

Calculating the exact value of each pip for the currency pair and lot size traded is the job of the broker's trading platform, which should include some kind of pip calculator created expressly for this purpose. In its absence, however, here is a simple calculation:

Value Per Pip = [Lot Size] × [Number of Lots] × [Pip Size]

The result of this equation will be denominated in the quote currency (the second currency in the pair). No currency conversion is needed for U.S. dollar-denominated trading accounts if the quote currency is already USD. To obtain the dollar value per pip if the quote currency is anything other than USD, however, the result must be converted to dollars using the current exchange rate between the quote currency and the U.S. dollar. Here are a few examples:

Example 1: Pip value for 1 standard lot of USD/JPY = 100,000 [Lot Size] × 1 [Number of Lots] × 000.01 [Pip Size] = ¥1000 (quote currency in Japanese yen)

Dollar pip value = ¥1000 ÷ 101.00 [current USD/JPY exchange rate] = $9.90/pip

Example 2: Pip value for 1 standard lot of EUR/GBP = 100,000 [Lot Size] × 1 [Number of Lots] × 0.0001 [Pip Size] = £10 (quote currency in British pounds)

Dollar pip value = £10 × 1.9750 [current GBP/USD exchange rate] = $ 19.75/pip

Example 3: Dollar pip value for 1 standard lot of EUR/USD = 100,000 [Lot Size] × 1 [Number of Lots] × 0.0001 [Pip Size] = $10/pip (quote currency already in U.S. dollars)

This may all seem very confusing at first to the beginning trader, but again, most forex trading platforms come well-equipped with a pip calculator that provides all pip values. If this calculator is not offered, it helps to keep in mind that all currency pairs ending in USD (as the quote currency) will be $10/pip for a standard lot,

$1/pip for a mini lot, and $0.10/pip for a micro lot. This includes heavily traded pairs like EUR/USD, GBP/USD, and AUD/USD.

For other key pairs like USD/JPY, USD/CHF, and USD/CAD, their exchange rates as of this writing conveniently place their pip values in the same approximate vicinity as the pairs ending in USD. For a standard lot, these pairs are currently at $9.87/pip, $9.99/pip, and $9.80/pip, respectively.

Finally, it should be kept in mind that while the lot size, amount of lots traded and specific currency pair traded will certainly affect pip value, the leverage chosen by the trader, whether it is 50:1, 400:1 or somewhere in between, has absolutely no bearing whatsoever on pip value.

Spreading the Wealth—Spreads or Commissions?

Closely related to pip value is the much-discussed topic of spreads. Futures and equities traders have been accustomed to paying commissions to their brokers on each and every trade, pretty much since the beginning of time. Within the past decade or so, retail foreign exchange brokers began emerging with their promises of no commissions.

Most recipients of this still-enduring marketing message eventually come to realize that the broker must somehow make money, if not through the "commissions" label. The moniker for forex broker revenue is therefore known as the *spread*.

A spread is simply the difference in pips between the bid price (exchange rate at which a trader can sell a currency pair) and the ask price (exchange rate at which a trader can buy a currency pair). Often, one may view an exchange rate quoted much like the following: 1.5850/53. This type of quote provides first the bid price and then the ask price as a variation of the bid. In this case, the two prices are separated by three pips.

These pips represent the spread, which is essentially the payment made to the broker for services rendered, in lieu of commissions. With most forex brokers, the spread is manifested immediately on trade entry. That is, once a trade is entered, whether it is a buy or sell, the open position immediately displays a running loss equivalent to the magnitude of the spread.

The spread deficit then needs to be overcome by favorable price movement before the trader can break even and have the opportunity to profit off the position. It should be made clear that this spread is charged only once on an entire trade cycle, from the open of the position to the close. Spreads are never charged twice on a single round-turn trade.

Most spreads on the major currency pairs, including EUR/USD, USD/JPY, GBP/USD, and USD/CHF, are usually in the vicinity of two to five pips wide. Looking back to the previous section on pip values, we can easily extrapolate the spread cost per trade.

For example, if trading one mini lot of EUR/USD, which may have a spread of 3 pips with a certain broker, the spread value for this trade would be USD $3.00 (as each pip on a EUR/USD mini lot is worth USD $1.00). This would constitute the primary transaction cost incurred for making the trade.

Generally speaking, spreads can either be variable or fixed. Many of the variable-spread brokers will advertise their tight spreads that prevail during quiet markets, but then widen the spreads considerably and without notice during the faster, more volatile markets. These faster markets usually occur around relatively frequent economic news announcements. Widened spreads during trading can potentially wreak havoc on open and/or pending positions. This could potentially include missed or prematurely triggered trade entries, stop losses, profit limits, or even margin calls.

Fixed-spread brokers, on the other hand, usually offer spreads that are slightly wider, but then actually keep those spreads fixed at a constant level, regardless of market conditions. This offers the clearly significant advantages of increased price certainty and fewer surprises. If a trader plans on ever buying and/or selling currencies during any type of fast market, it may perhaps be in the trader's best interest to choose a fixed-spread broker.

As for whether spreads or commissions are better, the jury is still out. As mentioned earlier, spreads and commissions both effectively represent a transactional payment by a customer for services offered by a broker. Assuming the amount is comparable, there is little difference beyond their labels. As of this writing, the vast majority of forex brokers continue to use the spread model, and this situation appears unlikely to change significantly within the near-term, foreseeable future.

Interest—Giving and Receiving

Though spreads are certainly the primary transactional cost in foreign exchange trading, there can also be a secondary cost that depends upon the currency pair traded, direction of the trade, and length of time the position is held. Interestingly enough, this potential second-ary cost can either be avoided altogether or even turned into a high-yielding positive. In foreign exchange trading, this phenomenon is known variously as "swap," "cost of carry," or simply "interest."

There is actually an entire trading strategy called *carry trading* that is based on earning highly leveraged, high-yield interest returns through holding strategic currency positions. This method will be discussed in-depth in Chapter 5, which covers specific trading strategies.

For now, though, a simple example will help illustrate the con-cept of interest in foreign exchange trading. At the time of this writ-ing, the Reserve Bank of Australia shows a relatively high central bank interest rate for the Australian dollar at 7.25%. The Bank of Japan, on the other hand, has kept the rate on the yen very low at 0.50%. The differential between these two rates (6.75%) is where the potential opportunity, as well as the potential cost, resides.

As described towards the beginning of this chapter in the section "Going Long and Selling Short," if a trader buys the AUD/JPY pair, that trader is essentially buying the Australian dollar (with the cur-rently high interest rate) while simultaneously selling the Japanese yen (with the currently low interest rate). The net effect is that the position would earn the high rate while paying the low rate. This creates a net-positive interest yield for the trader that is approxi-mately based on the rate differential between the two currencies. In this AUD/JPY example, the yield is based on the current 6.75% dif-ferential (minus an interest spread cost).

Conversely, if the trader sells the AUD/JPY pair, that trader is essentially selling the Australian dollar while simultaneously buying the yen. The net effect is that the position would earn the low rate (JPY) while paying the high rate (AUD). This creates a net-negative interest deficit for the trader that is approximately based upon the rate differential between the two currencies. In this AUD/JPY example, the deficit is based upon the current 6.75% differential (plus an interest spread cost).

Usually, traders would hardly get excited about the prospect of earning or paying seemingly insignificant sums due to interest, especially within the fast-paced, volatile world of currency trading.

But an extremely key point here that does often succeed in exciting traders is that the interest earned or paid is based on the *leveraged* amount traded, and not just upon the trader's fractional margin amount. In other words, to use the same AUD/JPY example, differential-based interest is actually earned or paid on the leveraged A$100,000 in the standard lot (100:1) trade, and not just on the A$1000 that the trader puts up in margin to make the trade. This can have enormous implications for traders who routinely hold their positions open, as the potential profit or loss every day due to interest alone can be very substantial.

Whether the trader pays or earns the interest, it is calculated daily according to the leveraged net interest rate differential of the trader's open position(s), taking into account the inevitable interest rate spread cost. With most foreign exchange brokers, the daily amount paid or charged to the trader (depending on the direction of the position(s), long or short) is added to or subtracted from the trader's account each day when open positions get "rolled over" (as described in Chapter 1). This process generally occurs at the same time every trading day, and is usually at the end of each business day, but the specific time varies among the different foreign exchange brokers.

Whether a trader seeks to avoid interest charges, gain interest payments, or neither, it is extremely important to be aware of how interest may affect all foreign exchange positions.

Hedging—Two Sides of the Same Coin

The final topic for this chapter on basic foreign exchange trading mechanics may not be quite as basic as the other topics in this chapter. Hedging is a rather specialized trading function that not every trader utilizes. In fact, most foreign exchange brokers do not even offer it on their trading platforms. But if available, hedging can be a useful tool for those traders who have specific strategies for employing it.

To hedge is to be long and short in the same currency pair at the same time. For example, if a trader buys one lot of USD/JPY and sells one lot of USD/JPY at the same time, that trader can be said to be in a perfectly hedged trading situation that is completely profit/loss-neutral. In other words, any price movement in the currency pair—up, down, or sideways—would not exert the least bit of influence on a hedged trade.

So why, then, would a trader utilize a trading functionality that mimics not taking a position at all? Some traders have developed strategies—especially those geared toward exploiting news-driven price spikes—that involve the strategic use of hedging. For the majority of traders that do not employ hedging, though, it is sufficient at least to be aware that hedging exists, and that it can potentially be used for protecting a one-sided currency position.

Those brokers that do not offer hedging simply close the original one-sided position if an opposite position in the same currency pair is initiated. For the hedging brokers, however, opposite positions in the same currency pair are treated as two open positions that effectively cancel out each other's running profit/loss.

One final note about hedging is that since two exactly opposing positions are profit/loss-neutral, and therefore create essentially a riskless trading scenario, brokers that offer hedging usually require margin on only one side of the hedge. The other, opposing side is a margin-free trade. This means that none of the trader's trading equity needs to be used to open and sustain the second leg of a hedge.

Chapter Summary

Since currencies are always traded in pairs, their value is determined by the market on a relative basis rather than an absolute basis. In forex trading, one currency can only have value if it is compared and contrasted to another currency. Because of this fact that forex is all about trading one against another, both going long (buying) and selling short (selling) always involve betting on one currency while simultaneously betting against another. So being long EUR/USD means buying EUR while selling USD, and being short EUR/ USD means selling EUR while buying USD.

There are a few methods for entering into forex trades. A market order opens a trade at the current market price. An entry order places an order to open a trade if price reaches a certain level predetermined by the trader. Similar to the way trades are entered, they ed. This can be accomplished through manually clos-

, which is the exiting equivalent of the market order

rough predetermined stop losses and profit limits.

ors that affect trading significantly include lot size and leverage. Lot size is the actual amount that is being traded, while leverage is the degree to which a trader's financial power can be magnified in order to control more in a trade with less capital.

A margin call is a safety measure that occurs when a trader no longer possesses enough equity in the trading account to support open position(s). In this event, all open positions are automatically closed at the prevailing market rates, thereby preventing even further catastrophic account losses.

Pips are the smallest unit of currency movement, and they serve as the primary measure of profit or loss in currency trades. Spreads, which are the main transaction cost incurred by traders when trading with the vast majority of forex brokers, are measured in pips. A spread is simply the difference between the price at which a currency pair is bought and the price at which it is sold. This difference, which varies with each broker, is automatically deducted once from each round-turn trade (open and close).

Interest represents another potential cost of trading, although traders may also earn interest on their trading positions. Depending on the specific currency pair and the direction in which it is traded (long or short), interest can either represent a significant expense on positions that are held overnight, or a way to generate daily income from holding open trades.

Finally, hedging is a more advanced topic that involves the simultaneous buying and selling of the same currency pair at the same time. When implemented, this creates a situation where any exchange rate movement will not affect the profit/loss picture, since one side of the hedge profits as the other side loses by an equal amount.

After this discussion on basic foreign exchange trading mechanics, the next logical step is to explore the features and functionalities of a currency trading platform. This can be accomplished at no cost simply by signing up for a free demo practice account with any reputable online forex broker. The best part about this is that a forex trader can test-drive a trading platform in an extremely thorough manner, secure in the knowledge that all losses in a practice account are not only free-of-charge, but also highly educational.

CHAPTER 3

Technical Analysis— Tools for Trading Foreign Exchange

After reading this chapter, you will be able to:

- Apply the primary tools used by technical traders to analyze the foreign exchange markets.

- Understand the purposes and mechanics of the most important functional elements of currency charts.

- Delve into the most practical aspects of technical analysis, including pattern recognition, drawing trendlines, and identifying support and resistance.

Introduction to Technical Analysis— Interpreting Price Action

Technical analysis is the most popular discipline, or school of financial analysis, for trading the foreign exchange markets. Simply put, technical analysis is often defined as the systematic study of price action, which is ultimately derived from the effects of mass market behavior.

While fundamental analysis may concern itself with the myriad reasons *why* price moves, technical analysis is single-mindedly focused on *how* price moves, and the ways in which that might affect future price movement. Technical analysis consists of a broad methodology through which traders can make all of their most important trading decisions. This includes entries, exits, stop-loss placement, profit target placement, trade-sizing, risk management, and more.

The primary toolbox used by foreign exchange technical analysts in analyzing and interpreting price action is the versatile currency chart. As we shall soon see, there are several styles of these toolboxes, including bar charts, candlestick charts, and point & figure charts.

Furthermore, within each of these toolboxes is quite a diverse set of tools. These tools can range anywhere from a simple trendline to an elaborate chart pattern to a mathematically derived oscillator to a complex algorithmic trading system. For the purposes of this book, however, we will stick to the essentials.

When a beginner is first introduced to using technical analysis for analyzing and trading the foreign exchange markets, there are invariably several buzzwords and phrases that are heard most frequently. These include such common terms as trend, support/ resistance, moving averages, head-and-shoulders pattern, Fibonacci, Elliott Wave, and so on. All of these terms, and much more, will be addressed further on in this chapter.

In the actual practice of technical analysis, however, generally it is better to keep all of these countless chart elements to a manageable minimum in order to avoid the very common beginner's epidemic of "paralysis by analysis." This is where traders clutter their charts with so many lines and indicators that they become utterly unable to conduct any useful analysis or to act on any bonafide signals from their charts. In the world of technical analysis, too much of a good thing is just as bad as the opposite extreme of not enough.

To avoid paralysis by analysis, traders should ideally master a handful of chart elements and become an expert on how price reacts to these elements. For example, a trader may study in-depth how a certain currency pair reacts over time in relation to the outer bands of the popular Bollinger Bands indicator. Or another trader may wish to become an expert on price behavior around the key Fibonacci retracement levels. Yet another trader may choose to work exclusively with trendlines, trading bounces and breakouts of these dynamic support/resistance levels. There is virtually no end to how a technical analyst may specialize to become a master of one (or a few), rather than an unfocused Jack of all Trades.

The primary advantages of technical analysis for the foreign exchange trader are manifold. This includes the exceptionally precise trade entries and exits afforded by chart analysis, sensible risk management through the use of technically derived stop levels, the ability to backtest technical strategies using past price action, and the unambiguous, rule-based nature of many technical trading systems. These concepts will all be covered in this chapter and in Chapter 5, which covers trading methods and strategies.

While technical analysis can be a powerful method for analyzing foreign exchange price movement, it can also be both time-consuming and incredibly frustrating. This is often the case when indicators or lines that traders rely upon to provide them with profitable trading signals give false signals, conflicting signals, or just plain don't work. But this should not be a valid reason to abandon the entire discipline of technical analysis altogether. As alluded to previously, there is no lack of foreign exchange traders who, through untiring study and experience, have managed to build successful trading careers from specializing in just a handful of technical methods that work well for them.

Therefore, patience and the careful study of technical tools and methods clearly comprise the path to mastery of technical analysis. In turn, the mastery of technical analysis may well provide the road to consistent profitability in the foreign exchange markets.

Basics of Bars and Candlesticks

Bars and candlesticks are the primary building blocks of technical analysis charting. There are several other methods of depicting price action visually in the foreign exchange markets, including older techniques that enjoy significant followings like point & figure charts (which will be touched on later in this chapter), but bars and candlesticks have assumed their vital roles as the main workhorses of present-day technical analysis.

Bar charts and candlestick charts share close similarities in that they both represent the most salient data points available in price action analysis. Within a given time period, this includes the open price, the high price, the low price, and the close price. For example, a daily chart, where each bar or candlestick represents one full trading day, will depict the price levels at which a given day opened and closed, as well as the high and low that were reached during that day. In the foreign exchange markets, incidentally, a trading day would consist of a full 24 hours. Exhibit 3.1 shows an example of both a bar and a candlestick.

As shown in Exhibit 3.1, a bar opens at the level of the left horizontal arm and closes at the level of the right horizontal arm. The top of the vertical bar represents that period's high, while the bottom represents the low.

In contrast, a candlestick places much heavier emphasis on the open and close of a particular period by making the space between

EXHIBIT 3.1

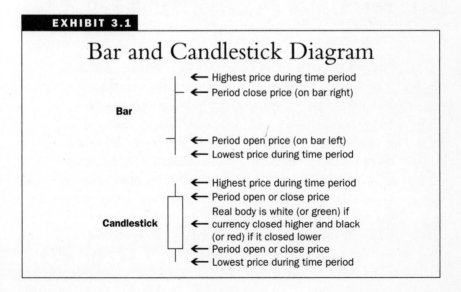

Bar and Candlestick Diagram

Bar

← Highest price during time period
← Period close price (on bar right)

← Period open price (on bar left)
← Lowest price during time period

Candlestick

← Highest price during time period
← Period open or close price
Real body is white (or green) if
← currency closed higher and black
(or red) if it closed lower
← Period open or close price
← Lowest price during time period

the open and close exceptionally prominent. This space is called the "real body." The vertical lines above and below are called "shadows" or "wicks." If the real body is white (or green), it means that it was a bullish candle, and that price opened at the bottom of the real body and closed at the top of the real body. If, on the other hand, the real

EXECUTIVE INSIGHT

Steve Nison

The most authoritative voice on the subject of candlesticks would certainly be Steve Nison, CMT. But besides having introduced the entire concept of Japanese candlesticks to the English-speaking world, Nison has also been a renowned expert on Western-style technical analysis for over three decades. Therefore, he brings a unique perspective that straddles both Eastern and Western methods of charting. Widely quoted in the major financial press as one of the world's foremost technical analysts, Nison authored the definitive book on the subject of candlesticks, *Japanese Candlestick Charting Techniques*, and is the founder and President of CandleCharts.com.

Nison states:

"Warren Buffett said he would be a bum in the street with a tin cup if the markets were always efficient. And why aren't the markets efficient? It's because of human emotions such as fear, greed, and hope. And the only way to gauge the emotional and psychological aspects of market participants is technical analysis. Bernard Baruch, one of most famous economists of the 20th century stated, 'It's not the news itself, but it is the market's reaction to the news that's important.' And for those who watch the forex market we know that many times an ounce of emotion can be worth a pound of facts.

The reason I'm spending time on the importance of market psychology is that the candlesticks—which I refer to as candles—is one of the best methods to get a quick visual grasp of who's winning in the ongoing battle of the bulls versus the bears. While very easy to construct, the candles provide an x-ray into the supply/demand situation. As the Japanese proverb states, 'Look at the outside and know the inside.' Think about the candle line. A tall white real body means the bulls are in charge during that session—whether it's an intraday, daily, or weekly. A long black real body hints the bears are in force. A doji (where the open and close are the same) clearly reflects a market in balance between the bulls and bears. And if a doji emerges during a rally, it increases the chances of a turn. A hammer, with its extended long lower shadow, is visually proving the market is rejecting lower levels. So on this one session it means that the bears are getting less confident because the market can't hold the lows into the close, while the bulls are getting more optimistic. In essence, the candlestick line is drawn based on the psychological underpinning of current market activity. And by reading the candles correctly you are reading the market's message.

As the author mentions in this chapter, I recommend using candles as just one of the tools in a trading arsenal. However, after you gain the knowledge of how to correctly and fully harness the insight of the candles you'll find that they will become one of your most important tools. At my live seminars, where I have taught thousands of retail and institutional traders, I often ask at the conclusion, 'Who would ever go back to a bar chart?' No one has ever raised a hand."

body is black (or red), it means that it was a bearish candle, and that price opened at the top of the real body and closed at the bottom of the real body.

In both the U.S. equities and futures markets, bar charts have traditionally been the primary mode of representing price action for technical analysis purposes. Only in the past decade or so have candlestick charts come into popular usage in the Western world, largely through the efforts of Steve Nison, who introduced this ancient charting method to America from its humble rice-trading roots in Japan.

The main difference between bars and candlesticks lies in their differing visual portrayals of identical price data points. Therefore, although both charting methodologies utilize the same data, which includes the open, high, low, and close price of a given time period, the manner in which this information is represented differs significantly between the two. While bars may reveal all of the usual support/resistance indications and chart patterns that Western technical analysts normally look for, candlesticks go a step further by including all of this relevant information plus providing a unique visual interpretation of the struggle between bulls (buyers) and bears (sellers).

Furthermore, while there are numerous popular chart patterns that are commonly associated with bar charts (e.g., head-and-shoulder, double tops, triangles, flags, and pennants, among many others), candlestick charts include all of these formations, plus incorporate an additional library of imaginatively named chart patterns like "morning star," "hammer," and "hanging man," among many others. All of these patterns for both bar and candlestick charts will be explained later in this chapter.

Keeping Time with Chart Timeframes

While the structures of bars and candlesticks are relatively straight-forward, these stick shapes would mean very little from an analytical perspective without the vital element of time. On both bar and candlestick charts, the vertical *y*-axis represents the price of one currency in a pair against the other, while the horizontal *x*-axis represents time moving forward from left to right. This is illustrated in Exhibit 3.2.

Point & figure (p&f) charts are the notable exception to this prevailing axis structure, as they do not include the time element. But these unique p&f charts will be touched upon in more detail later on in this chapter.

EXHIBIT 3.2

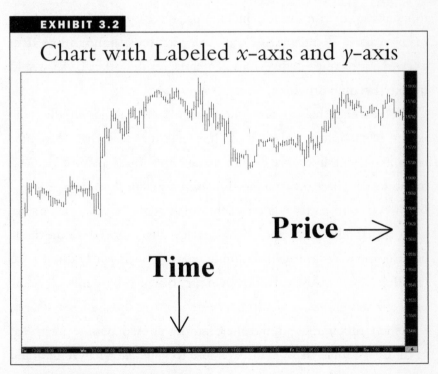

Chart with Labeled *x*-axis and *y*-axis

Source: FX Solutions – FX AccuCharts

Most charting software allows traders to choose from a wide variety of timeframes for bar and candlestick charts. This choice is critical for numerous reasons. Most importantly, it dictates how much time is contained in each bar or candlestick. For example, in a daily chart, each bar has a duration of exactly one day, or 24 hours. A five-minute candlestick, on the other hand, has a duration of exactly five minutes. It is crucial for traders to know exactly what timeframe is being viewed at all times, as there are differing strategies for long-term, medium-term, and short-term trading.

Another reason that the timeframe holds so much importance is that it determines how much price action can practically be viewed at one time. Longer-term charts like daily, weekly, and monthly timeframes can comfortably include price action visuals going back many years or decades. Displaying price action spanning more than a few days for one- or five-minute charts, on the other hand, would quickly become unwieldy.

Yet another reason timeframes are so critical lies in the very nature of technical analysis itself. It is certainly true that chart patterns are generally fractal, which means that these patterns can be found on all chart timeframes. But from a practical trading perspective, trends and patterns are usually much more reliable on longer-term charts like daily and higher, rather than shorter-term charts like the intraday hourly and minute charts. This is partly due to the fact that directionless volatility, or noise, that usually defies all technical analysis efforts, is much more prevalent on shorter-term charts.

Chart timeframes should therefore be chosen with a great deal of care. Of course, many traders choose to view and analyze multiple timeframes simultaneously in order to identify trend confirmations and/or conflicts. This type of trading approach will be discussed in Chapter 5, which covers trading methods and strategies.

Popular timeframes used by foreign exchange traders include (in ascending order of duration): 1-minute, 5-minute, 10-minute, 15-minute, 30-minute, 1-hour, 2-hour, 3-hour, 4-hour, 12-hour, daily, weekly, and monthly. There are also multitick timeframes, where each bar or candlestick contains a certain number of ticks (minimum incremental movements in price), but these are not nearly as popular as the abovementioned standard duration timeframes.

Support for Resistance (and Support)

Now that basic chart structure has been established, the real "meat and potatoes" of technical analysis can be discussed, and there is no better place to begin than with support and resistance. Besides the notion of trend, which will be discussed in the next section, the twin concepts of support and resistance are at the core of technical analysis. Their explanation is rather simple, yet their significance is far-reaching.

Support and resistance are two parts of one whole. They can also be considered polar opposites. Support is simply defined as the recurring upward price "pressure" found at relatively lower prices, while resistance is the recurring downward price "pressure" found at relatively higher prices. These upward and downward pressures have a number of hypothetical causes, many of which are purported to relate closely with mass trader psychology.

Without delving into the theoretical underpinnings of the collective trader psyche, however, the concepts of support and resistance are often considered simply to stem from market participants' price memory, among other factors. This idea will be explored briefly here.

From a price memory perspective, sustainable support and resistance levels will occur because traders remember specific price levels, and will base their trading decisions on whether they consider these levels as relatively high or relatively low. The most basic tendency is for traders to buy at price levels they consider relatively low (support) and to sell at price levels they consider relatively high (resistance).

When a majority of traders collectively believe that a certain price level or region is relatively low, buying pressure will often result and the price should generally go up, thereby creating a "bounce up off support." Conversely, when a majority of traders believe that a certain price level or region is relatively high, selling pressure will often result and the price should generally go down, thereby creating a "bounce down off resistance."

For an example of resistance, if the price region surrounding 1.6000 on the EUR/USD is considered collectively by traders to be relatively high (which, as of this writing, is the case), traders without positions in the market may wish to sell short the pair if this level is reached, with the intention to profit by buying back (or covering) later at a lower price. By the same token, traders with existing long positions in the pair may also wish to sell at this level, effectively closing their positions and taking their profits. All of this selling activity places downward pressure at this 1.6000 level, thereby creating significant resistance in the form of a "ceiling" on price action. The expectation, then, is that when price reaches a significant resistance level, it will turn and go back down at that level.

If, on the other hand, the price region surrounding 95.00 on the USD/JPY is considered collectively by traders to be relatively low, traders without positions in the market may wish to buy the pair if this level is reached, with the intention to profit by selling their positions later at a higher price. And traders with existing short positions in the pair may also wish to buy back (or cover) at this level, effectively closing their positions and taking their profits. All of this buying activity places upward pressure at this 95.00 level, thereby creating significant support in the form of a "floor" on price action. The expectation, then, is that when price reaches a significant support level, it will turn and go back up at that level.

Sideways price action between both a support floor and a resistance ceiling is called a trading range, as displayed in Exhibit 3.3. These occur quite often in the foreign exchange markets. Many currency traders exploit breakouts or breakdowns of low volatility trading ranges as one of their primary trade entry tactics. This will be discussed further in Chapter 5, which covers trading methods and strategies.

The simple fact that support and resistance levels are often respected by price numerous times before ultimately being broken is, in itself, a remarkable phenomenon that can contribute a great deal to any foreign exchange trader's strategy. Therefore, whenever price nears historically significant support or resistance levels, traders and analysts will invariably begin paying close attention to the

EXHIBIT 3.3

Trading Range Support and Resistance

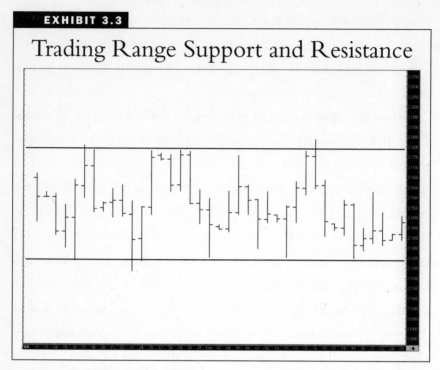

Source: FX Solutions – FX AccuCharts

action, waiting for the level in question either to be respected or broken. These traders and analysts will then act accordingly.

Another important aspect of traders' collective price memory as it relates to the concept of support and resistance lies in the extraordinary tendency for a support/resistance level to transform into the opposite, once broken. For example, when price breaks out above a previous resistance level, technical analysts and traders would then consider that broken resistance level as a new support level. By the same token, when price breaks down below a previous support level, technical analysts and traders would then consider that broken support level as a new resistance level.

The most plausible reason for this phenomenon, from a technical analysis perspective, is that once a currency pair breaks a support/resistance level in a convincing manner, traders begin to believe that the pair has reached a whole new plateau of price activity. Therefore, mass trader momentum will move away from the previous price level, towards equilibrium at this new norm. The border between the old plateau and the new one is the broken support/resistance zone, and it will therefore be expected to act as a future price barrier.

For example, if the GBP/USD breaks out and remains above a highly significant resistance level that represents a multidecade high, say at 2.1160 (as of this writing), traders will begin to believe that the pair will continue to move within this new, higher plateau. This is because it would be such a technically rare feat to break this lofty level that price must be trending up with extremely strong momentum. So when the level is finally broken, if price ever subsequently went back down to revisit that broken resistance line around 2.1160, it would signal a relatively low price, and therefore a good place to buy at support. And when a lot of major market participants all decide to buy at support, it can be manifested in price action as a bounce up off support. This phenomenon can be seen in Exhibit 3.4.

Of course, as with every aspect of technical analysis (or any other analysis, for that matter), this tendency does not always work out as expected. But the phenomenon is realized frequently enough in the foreign exchange markets to warrant serious consideration. The expectation that support becomes resistance, and resistance becomes support, is one of the central themes of the support/resistance concept, as well as of technical analysis as a whole.

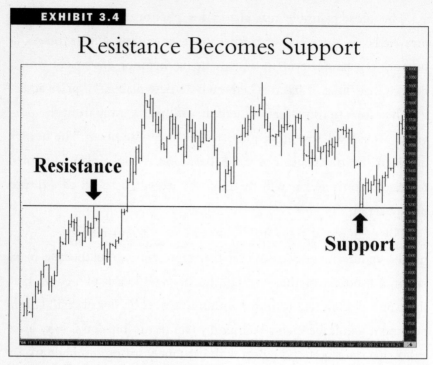

EXHIBIT 3.4

Resistance Becomes Support

Source: FX Solutions – FX AccuCharts

The Trend Will Set You Free

Even more important to the practice of technical analysis than support and resistance is the concept of trend. Knowing the trend at any given time is absolutely essential to analyzing charts effectively. Though this may appear to be a simple thing, there are plenty of nuances in identifying trends that make it an art unto itself.

One of the major complexities involved in determining whether the trend is up or down has to do with timeframes, as presented earlier in this chapter. On a long-term monthly bar chart of AUD/USD, for example, where each bar is the equivalent of one month of price action, the prevailing trend may be unmistakably up. At the same time, the medium-term daily chart might show that the current trend is down. In turn, the short-term hourly chart may be indicating an uptrend. And the ultra-short-term minute chart may be hinting at a downtrend. Up-down-up-down—which timeframe is indicating the correct trend direction for the currency pair?

The answer depends entirely upon which timeframe(s) a particular trader is accustomed to trading. It may well be true that the longer timeframes offer more reliable trend indications, as shorter timeframes tend to include a lot of market noise, or minor price fluctuations that have very little to do with the overall trend. At the same time, however, a short-term intraday trader might well be advised to ignore price action on the weekly chart entirely. The long-term trend is virtually irrelevant to the shortest-term intraday trader. Likewise, a long-term position trader can certainly ignore the intraday price movements on a 5-minute chart.

A potential method that can be used for dealing with trends and timeframes is to concentrate on the trend indicated by a timeframe 4–6 times longer than the one traded. For example, if a trader is accustomed to analyzing a 1-hour chart for trades, the 4-hour chart (4 times the length of the 1-hour chart) would be used to indicate the trend. And if a trader is accustomed to analyzing a 4-hour chart for trades, the daily chart (6 times the length of the 4-hour chart) would be used to indicate the trend. Finally, if a trader is accustomed to analyzing a daily chart for trades, the weekly chart (5 times the length of the daily chart) would be used to indicate the trend.

Once the overall, longer-term trend is identified, many foreign exchange traders wisely follow the oft-repeated dictum that all trades should always be in the direction of the prevailing trend. Although there are certainly a substantial number of successful countertrend technical traders in the foreign exchange markets, there are arguably more successful traders that are of the trend-following persuasion.

Besides the issue of timeframe-compatibility in identifying trends, the larger question remains as to how a trend is inherently defined. If price movement consisted of a straight line either up or down, identifying a trend would obviously be too simple. In reality, currency prices move around incessantly, often denying the technical analyst an easy trend read.

There are primarily three modes of price movement that can be readily identified. They are uptrend mode, downtrend mode, and nontrending (sideways) mode. Remember that in the foreign exchange markets, an uptrend is simultaneously an uptrend for the base currency (first currency in the pair) and a downtrend for the quote currency (second currency in the pair). Conversely, a downtrend for a currency pair is simultaneously a downtrend for the base currency and an uptrend for the quote currency. Because nontrending mode, by definition, is not an integral part of a discussion on trends, it will be disregarded here.

Ideally, an uptrend is characterized by progressively higher lows and higher highs in price. An ideal downtrend, conversely, is characterized by progressively lower highs and lower lows. A low is considered a point of reversal between a downmove and an upmove. A high is considered a point of reversal between an upmove and a downmove.

Trends can be measured and evaluated with a number of tools, including trendlines, trend channels, moving averages, Average Directional Index (ADX), Directional Movement Index (DMI),

Elliott Wave, and others. These will all be discussed later in this chapter.

Although there are certainly idealistic conditions for the formation of uptrends and downtrends, in practice it can be difficult to find sustained trends that conform perfectly to these requirements (higher lows and highs for uptrends, and lower highs and lows for downtrends). Much more frequently, traders and analysts find on their charts uptrends that are only required to hit higher lows, and downtrends that are only required to hit lower highs. Thus, we have the terms, uptrend support and downtrend resistance. By definition, these two concepts comprise the technical analysis supertool for evaluating trends—the trendline. In turn, the trendline comprises half of another vitally important tool in trend analysis—the parallel trend channel.

How Trendy—Lines and Channels

Besides the ubiquitous horizontal support and resistance lines touched upon earlier in this chapter, trendlines and channels remain among the most utilized weapons in the technical analysis arsenal. There are almost as many ways to draw trendlines as there are traders using them in their analysis. Over time, there have also emerged countless new methodologies for drawing and interpreting these lines. But the traditional manner of constructing trendlines remains clear and focused. One would connect progressively higher lows (at least two, but preferably more) for an uptrend, as in Exhibit 3.5. In a similar manner, one would connect progressively lower highs (at least two, but preferably more) for a downtrend, as in Exhibit 3.6.

EXHIBIT 3.5

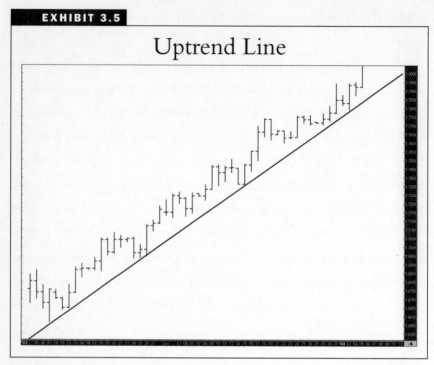

Uptrend Line

Source: FX Solutions – FX AccuCharts

The practical applications of trendlines can be enormously useful for the foreign exchange trader. In fact, there is a whole contingent of traders that prefers to use trendline analysis almost exclusively in dictating trading decisions. Trendlines can be used to pinpoint break-out entries, pullback entries, prudent stoplosses, and optimal profit targets. Though there can often be excessive subjectivity in their construction and interpretation, trendlines have withstood the test of time as an integral component of many of the most profitable trading strategies. These will be discussed in more detail in Chapter 5.

If a trendline supplies just the floor for an uptrend, the parallel uptrend channel provides the ceiling as well. By the same token, if a

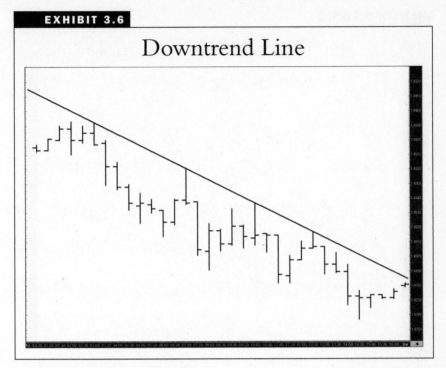

EXHIBIT 3.6

Downtrend Line

Source: FX Solutions – FX AccuCharts

trendline supplies just the ceiling for a downtrend, the parallel down-trend channel provides the floor as well. Price action that truly fits comfortably into the borders of a parallel trend channel upholds the highest ideals of a true trend. This is because, for example, an uptrend that fits well into a parallel uptrend channel will contain both higher lows *and* higher highs (see Exhibit 3.7). At the same time, a down-trend that fits well into a parallel downtrend channel will contain both lower highs *and* lower lows (see Exhibit 3.8). This is in contrast to the single trendline, which requires price only to fulfill half of the ideal.

One caveat regarding the parallel trend channel is that it often encourages traders to trade against the trend. In an uptrend channel,

EXHIBIT 3.7

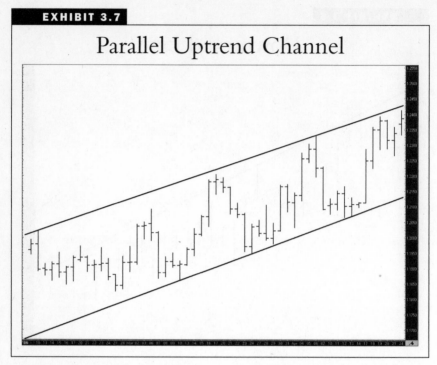

Parallel Uptrend Channel

Source: FX Solutions – FX AccuCharts

for example, with support on the bottom line and resistance on the top, many traders are tempted not only to enter long on the bottom, but also to enter short on the top. A long entry on the bottom of an uptrend channel is a trade in the direction of the trend, while a short entry at the top of that same uptrend channel is a countertrend trade. Though countertrend trading is by no means a taboo practice, and it can often prove to be a profitable trading style for experienced traders, it is probably best for newer traders to stick to trading with the trend. According to strict trendtraders, the top of an uptrend channel should be used exclusively for profit-taking on longs, rather than entering short trades against the direction of the trend.

EXHIBIT 3.8

Parallel Downtrend Channel

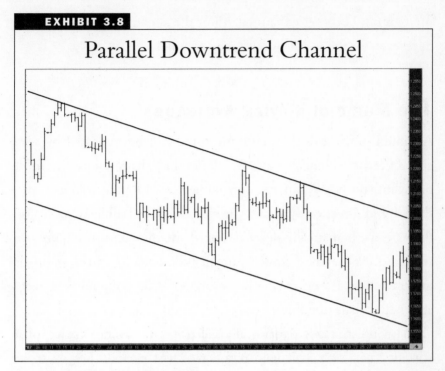

Source: FX Solutions – FX AccuCharts

Another word of caution regarding channels relates to breakouts. Many beginning traders will treat breakouts on both sides of a trend channel as similar events. This could not be further from the truth. In a parallel uptrend channel, for example, a breakdown below the uptrend support line represents a potential change in trend that is generally considered a highly significant and potentially actionable event. A breakout above the top line of the uptrend channel, on the other hand, is much less of an important or actionable event from a trading perspective. This type of breakout merely represents an acceleration of the trend, which frequently meets eventual failure as momentum becomes exhausted. All of the above also holds true, but in reverse, for the parallel downtrend channel.

The Magic of Moving Averages

As noted previously, the prevailing trend can be indicated by several different technical tools. Trendlines and channels are the most prevalent, but they can be very subjective. Moving averages also show trend direction well, and they are much less subjective because they are mathematically derived. Therefore, they do not require the trader to use nearly as much human judgment in construction or interpretation. By no means, however, does this make moving averages better than trendlines—they are just different.

Moving averages dynamically calculate the average price of a currency pair over a defined number of past periods. For example, on a daily chart (where each bar is worth one 24-hour period), a 20-period simple moving average (SMA) adds the daily close prices for the last 20 days and divides by 20. This calculation simply results in the average, or mean, price for the last 20 days. But when this average is continuously calculated every single day (hence the term "moving" in moving average), it results in a dynamic line that follows price, and can effectively describe the trend. Exhibit 3.9 shows a good example of a 20-period moving average expressing the overall trend.

One major weakness of moving averages that is often cited by traders and analysts is the fact that they invariably lag, or follow, price. Moving averages, therefore, can never be predictive, as price always arrives where it will arrive well before any moving average could.

EXHIBIT 3.9

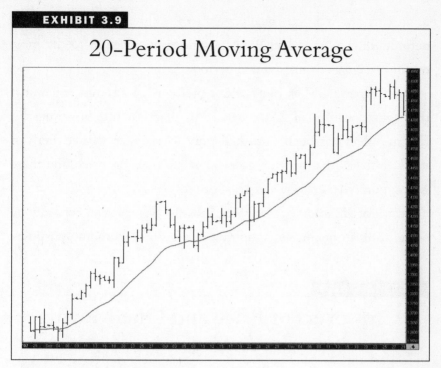

20-Period Moving Average

Source: FX Solutions – FX AccuCharts

Consequently, although moving averages can certainly do a good job of describing a current trend, they are extremely lacking when it comes to signaling changes in trends. Many analysts and traders throughout the decades have attempted to address this shortcoming by creating new ways of calculating these important indicators.

As a result, there are three primary types of moving averages that are in the most common use today, which are all distinct from each other by their mathematical constructs. The three types are as follows: the simple moving average (SMA), the weighted moving average (WMA), and the exponential moving average (EMA). Without delving into the source of their mathematical distinctions, suffice it to say that SMAs assign equal weight to all of the data in the defined period, while WMAs and EMAs assign greater weight to the most recent price data in the defined period.

WMAs and EMAs came about partly as an attempt to combat the lagging nature of SMA signals. In practical use, however, this lagging effect has been mitigated only to a minor degree. Perhaps it is safe to say that moving averages will always lag price, and there is not much that anyone can do about it.

Lag notwithstanding, however, moving averages can certainly be useful tools in helping to simplify price action for trading purposes.

EXHIBIT 3.10

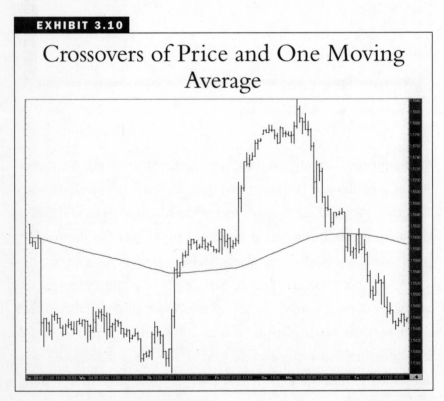

Crossovers of Price and One Moving Average

Source: FX Solutions – FX AccuCharts

This is accomplished primarily through the use of moving average crossovers. In the world of moving averages, a crossover can be defined in a number of different ways.

The most basic crossover, as shown in Exhibit 3.10, involves the intersection of price and a single moving average. If price crosses above the moving average, it would represent a possible opportunity to buy the currency pair. If, on the other hand, price crosses below the moving average, it would signify a possible sell, or short.

The second type of crossover, as shown in Exhibit 3.11, is probably the most commonly used moving average strategy. It involves the use of two moving averages of different periods, say 5 and 20,

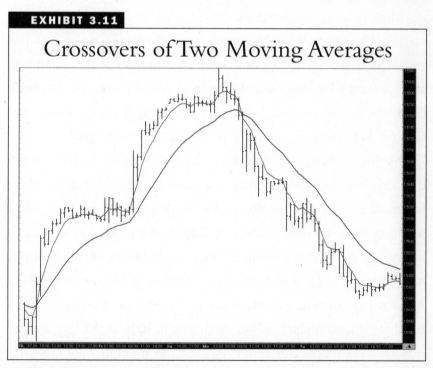

EXHIBIT 3.11

Crossovers of Two Moving Averages

Source: FX Solutions – FX AccuCharts

for example. If the shorter-period moving average crosses above the longer one, it would be considered a signal to buy. Conversely, if the shorter moving average crosses below the longer one, it would be considered a signal to sell.

The third primary type of moving average crossover involves the use of three moving averages. This method of using multiple confirming lines attempts to help combat the unprofitable whipsaw action that often results from nontrending, sideways markets. Systems using three different moving averages usually produce signals when the shortest period moving average crosses both longer moving averages, or when the shortest moving average crosses the middle one and then the middle one subsequently crosses the longest.

Most moving average trading systems are generally always in the market. This means that after each trade is opened on a crossover and then closed on an opposite crossover, another trade is immediately opened in the opposite direction to take the place of the previous trade. Therefore, there is always at least one trade open, whether long or short, depending on the prevailing crossover signal.

As just mentioned, beginning traders should be forewarned that although crossover signals can often be exceptionally profitable, those traders that use them must be prepared for frequent losses resulting from common whipsaw action. Whipsaws occur regardless of however many moving averages and confirmation crossovers happen to be utilized in a given trading system. The most common whipsaws occur when crossovers occur incessantly because of nontrending, sideways price action (as shown in Exhibit 3.12). This type of price choppiness almost always results in multiple false crossover signals with little to no follow-through, and consequently a string of

EXHIBIT 3.12

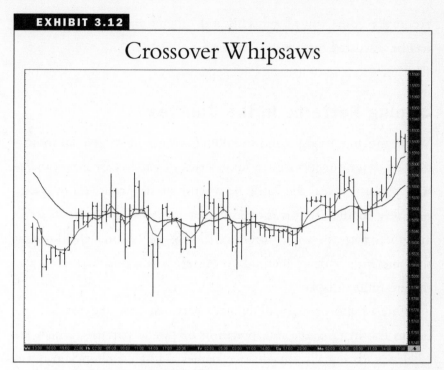

Crossover Whipsaws

Source: FX Solutions – FX AccuCharts

many small losses. Like its close cousin, the lag, the whipsaw is simply an unavoidable fact of trading with moving averages.

The idea behind moving average trading methods, therefore, centers on the goal of gaining large profits during trending periods when crossovers are few and far between—while at the same time withstanding the inevitable small losses during sideways whipsaw periods when crossovers are abundant. The greatest challenge with this type of trading lies in the ability of the trader to let the winning trades run while immediately closing losing trades. Only in this way can a trader using moving averages profit enough during trends to offset the many losses incurred during horizontal price activity, and eventually come out ahead. This and other trend-trading strategies will be discussed further in Chapter 5.

Seeing Patterns in the Candles

While moving averages and trendlines are meant to give an indication of trend direction for a long series of candles or bars, candlestick patterns reveal the battle between bulls and bears on only one or a few candles. As mentioned earlier in this chapter, candlesticks and their patterns were introduced by Steve Nison, who brought this ancient charting method to America from its humble rice-trading roots in Japan.

One of the primary differences between bars and candlesticks lies in the imaginative interpretation of candle patterns, which are labeled with equally imaginative names. Most candlestick patterns are considered either price reversal formations or patterns indicating indecision, while only a few are considered trend continuation formations.

Before moving onto a presentation of the most common and important candlestick patterns developed in Japan, it should be noted that these patterns were never meant to comprise a complete trading system. Rather, most high-level practitioners of candlestick analysis, including Nison himself, state emphatically that candle patterns are intended either to confirm or be confirmed by other technical studies. In other words, candle patterns should not be relied upon exclusively to provide the full technical picture. That being said, candle patterns can contribute a great deal of insight to any technician's analytical process.

Following are illustrations and explanations of some of the most common candlestick patterns found in the foreign exchange markets. Several patterns, like the morning star and evening star, are omitted because of their relative lack of compatibility with currency charts. In this case, a morning/evening star depends on a gap between candle opens/closes, which, in the 24-hour foreign exchange market, is relatively rare.

Exhibit 3.13 illustrates the most common single-candle patterns used in forex trading.

A doji forms when a currency pair's open and close are either equal or close to equal. After the doji opens, price may go up and/or down substantially, but should close at or near the open price. This pattern represents indecision, or a tug-of-war, between the pair's buyers and sellers. Only with additional technical confirmation could a doji be considered the beginnings of a price reversal.

EXHIBIT 3.13

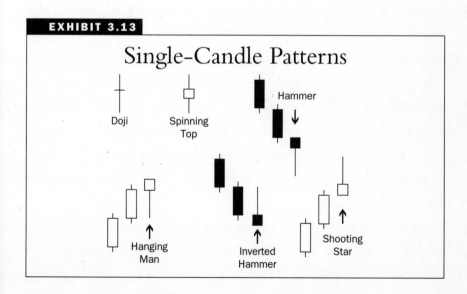

Single-Candle Patterns

Doji

Spinning Top

Hammer

Hanging Man

Inverted Hammer

Shooting Star

Another sign of indecision similar to the doji is the spinning top. A spinning top has a very small real body with upper and lower shadows that are longer than the length of the real body.

Hammers occur after downtrends, and signify a potential reversal. A hammer is top-heavy with the real body, and has a long lower shadow. The color of the real body is not important.

A hanging man looks identical to a hammer, but occurs after an uptrend. Just like the hammer, a hanging man is top-heavy with the real body, and has a long lower shadow. It also signifies a potential reversal, and the color of the real body is unimportant.

An inverted hammer is naturally the opposite of a hammer. Like the hammer, the inverted hammer also occurs after downtrends, signifies a potential reversal, and has a body color that is not vital to the integrity of the pattern. However, an inverted hammer looks like an upside-down hammer in that it is bottom-heavy with the real body, and has a long upper shadow.

In a similar manner, a shooting star is the opposite of a hanging man. Like the hanging man, the shooting star also occurs after uptrends, signifies a potential reversal, and has a body color that is not vital to the integrity of the pattern. However, a shooting star looks like an upside-down hanging man in that it is bottom-heavy with the real body, and has a long upper shadow.

With the most common single-candle patterns in forex covered, Exhibit 3.14 illustrates the most common multiple-candle patterns used in forex trading.

The bullish engulfing pattern is a bullish reversal pattern that usually occurs after a downtrend. Unlike the single-candle patterns described above, the bullish engulfing pattern is a two-candle pattern.

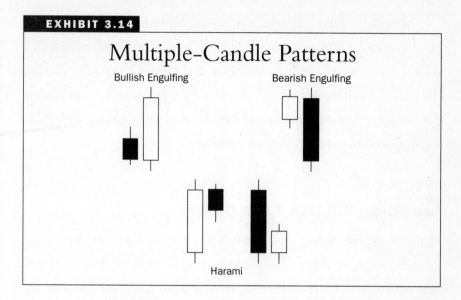

EXHIBIT 3.14

Multiple-Candle Patterns

Bullish Engulfing

Bearish Engulfing

Harami

It consists of a small bearish body on the first candle, followed by a large bullish body on the next candle that completely encompasses the small body's vertical range. This is considered a significant downtrend reversal pattern.

Like the bullish engulfing pattern, the bearish engulfing pattern is also a reversal pattern. However, a bearish engulfing pattern usually occurs after an uptrend. It consists of a small bullish body on the first candle, followed by a large bearish body on the next candle that completely encompasses the small body's vertical range. This is considered a significant uptrend reversal pattern.

The opposite of an engulfing pattern is a harami, which consists of a large body followed by a smaller, encompassed body of the opposite color. Therefore, a harami can either be a large bullish candle followed by a small bearish candle, or a large bearish candle followed by a small bullish candle. Like engulfing patterns, haramis are also considered reversal indicators.

Of course, there are many other multiple-candle patterns. But as mentioned previously, some depend upon gaps between candles, which are relatively rare in the 24-hour foreign exchange market. The basic candlestick patterns described in this chapter occur often on currency charts, and are therefore the best starting place for learning and practicing candlestick analysis.

Currency Charts Take Shape

Unlike candlestick patterns, traditional Western chart patterns usually take the form of shapes that develop over a relatively long series of bars or candles. Some of these shapes have been analyzed and traded by technical analysts almost since the advent of financial charting. Commonly, when most people think of charts and technical analysis, they often think of perhaps the most popular pattern, head-and-shoulders. Although the head-and-shoulders formation can be a solid, reliable pattern, there are a whole host of other potentially profitable patterns that many traders use on an extensive basis.

Chart patterns can be classified by their most common role, whether as a continuation pattern or a reversal pattern. Of course, a continuation pattern will not always act as a continuation pattern. It may sometimes act as a reversal pattern. The same is true for patterns that are commonly considered reversal patterns. But for the purposes of classification, these patterns can be divided according to their most common behavior.

For the vast majority of chart patterns, the technical analyst or trader looks either for breakouts to the upside or breakdowns to the downside. Once these patterns are broken, it is usually considered a trigger to trade in the direction of the break. Often, the break is false, and price will quickly return into the pattern from whence it broke. But that is where proper risk management comes in. It is easy to know where to place a stop loss on a break of a pattern. Wherever the break is deemed false or no longer valid (usually back on the side before the break), is where the stop loss should be placed. This will be explained further in the section of Chapter 6 on risk management.

The basic structure of the most common chart patterns in foreign exchange trading will be described here. Further information on trading chart patterns can be found in Chapter 5.

To begin with, Exhibit 3.15 shows illustrations of the most common reversal patterns.

Double tops and bottoms are both considered classic reversal formations. As its name implies, the double top occurs when price hits the same or similar price high twice consecutively after a major uptrend. The two peaks are separated by a trough. The signal to

EXHIBIT 3.15

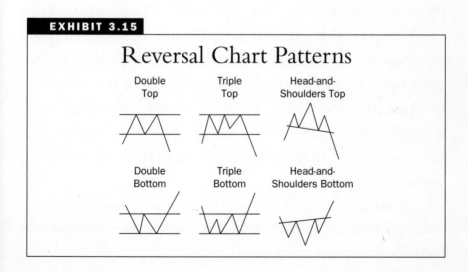

Reversal Chart Patterns

Double Top · Triple Top · Head-and-Shoulders Top

Double Bottom · Triple Bottom · Head-and-Shoulders Bottom

sell short comes on a subsequent breakdown of the lowest point in the trough (support). The double bottom occurs when price hits the same or similar price low twice consecutively after a major downtrend. The two troughs are separated by a peak. The signal to buy comes on a subsequent breakout of the highest point in the peak (resistance).

Triple tops and bottoms are also considered classic reversal formations. The triple top occurs when price hits the same or similar price high three times consecutively after a major uptrend. The peaks are separated by troughs. The signal to sell short comes on a subsequent breakdown of the lowest trough (support). The triple bottom occurs when price hits the same or similar price low three times consecutively after a major downtrend. The troughs are separated by peaks. The signal to buy comes on a subsequent breakout of the highest peak (resistance).

The well-known head-and-shoulders reversal pattern is similar to the triple top/bottom patterns. The primary difference lies in the middle of the pattern. For example, in a head-and-shoulders top, the middle peak (the head) is higher than the other two peaks (the shoulders). In an inverted head-and-shoulders bottom, on the other hand, the middle trough (the head) is lower than the other two troughs (the shoulders). The line connecting the troughs in a head-and-shoulders top, or the peaks in a head-and-shoulders bottom, is called the *neckline*. Breaks of this neckline are considered trading signals.

Following are some of the most common continuation patterns found on currency charts. Exhibit 3.16 displays the ubiquitous flag and pennant patterns.

EXHIBIT 3.16

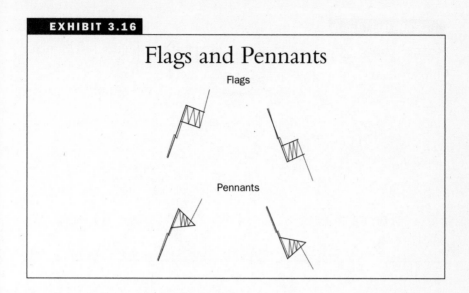

Flags and Pennants

Flags

Pennants

A flag is usually a smaller, shorter-term continuation pattern that is characterized by a sharp move followed by a rectangle consolidation, and then by a continuation of the move prior to the flag. Trades are signaled at the breakout/breakdown of the flag rectangle. Flags are very common on foreign exchange charts.

A pennant is very similar to a flag in that it is also generally a smaller, shorter-term continuation pattern. But after the initial sharp move, the pennant forms a small triangle consolidation. This should then be followed by a continuation of the move prior to the pennant. Trades are signaled at the breakout/breakdown of the pennant triangle. Like flags, pennants are also very common on currency charts.

Also generally considered continuation patterns, the primary triangle variations are displayed in Exhibit 3.17.

Triangles are larger price consolidation patterns that are characterized by progressively decreasing volatility as the pattern develops.

EXHIBIT 3.17

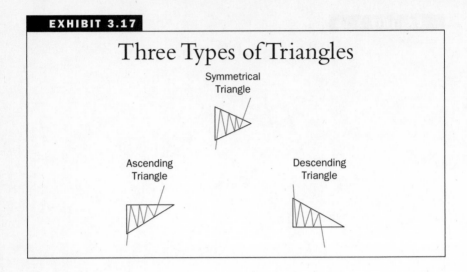

Three Types of Triangles

These common formations are most often considered continuation patterns. Symmetrical triangles are characterized by converging sides, where neither of these sides is flat, or horizontal. Trades are initiated at the triangle break.

Ascending triangles are also common continuation patterns, but they are most often considered bullish. As such, they usually form during uptrends as bullish continuation formations. An ascending triangle is characterized by a rising bottom line with a horizontal top line. A breakout above the top resistance line in an ascending triangle is considered a potential signal to buy.

Descending triangles are continuation patterns that are most often considered bearish. As such, they usually form during downtrends as bearish continuation formations. A descending triangle is characterized by a falling top line with a horizontal bottom line. A breakdown below the bottom support line in a descending triangle is considered a potential signal to sell short.

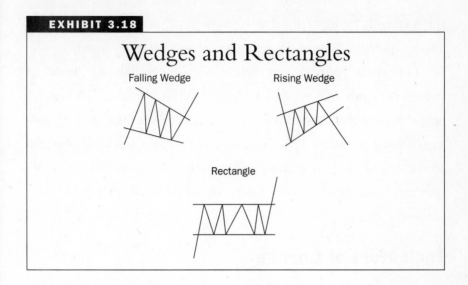

EXHIBIT 3.18

Wedges and Rectangles

Falling Wedge

Rising Wedge

Rectangle

Somewhat like symmetrical triangles, wedges are characterized by two converging lines, as shown in Exhibit 3.18. Unlike symmetrical triangles, however, the two sides of a wedge will both slope in the same direction. Therefore, a rising wedge will have two sides that both slope up, while a falling wedge will have two sides that both slope down. Falling wedges after uptrends are considered bullish continuation patterns, while rising wedges after downtrends are considered bearish continuation patterns. Trading signals are triggered on the breakout or breakdown of the wedge.

Similar to a parallel trend channel, but flat, a rectangle is a horizontal trading range bounded by two horizontal lines, as shown in Exhibit 3.18. Rectangles frequently serve as pauses in a trend, and therefore are often considered continuation patterns. At least two touches on both the top and bottom of a rectangle are necessary for the formation. Trades are signaled on the breakout or breakdown of the rectangle. Incidentally, if a rectangle is of sufficient height it can also be traded as a range, long at support and short at resistance.

The chart patterns just described are certainly far from an exhaustive study of technical trading patterns. However, they represent the most important and most common patterns found on foreign exchange charts. Therefore, they comprise a solid introduction to the world of chart pattern analysis. More information on strategies involving these patterns will be discussed in Chapter 5.

Indicators of Change

No discussion of technical analysis tools would be complete without mentioning some of the many mathematically derived indicators that seem to have proliferated through the years. New indicators appear all the time, promising to be the next miracle add-on to our price charts. Up to now, though, there have been very few, if any, miracles.

The main issue with many of these indicators is that, for the most part, they are lagging reflections of price. In other words, indicators are great at describing what price has done in the past, but since they mostly just follow price action, many indicators are hard-pressed to provide any reliable clue as to what might happen next. This was discussed earlier in this chapter in the section on moving averages, which are also considered lagging indicators. For this reason, many indicators are relegated to serving as secondary confirmation tools. Of course, it is true that no technical tool could ever really tell the future. But many of the indicators that novice traders love to clutter up their charts with are not much more than a repackaged version of price itself.

That being said, there are some very useful indicators available that can be extremely valuable in augmenting price action analysis. Some of these are described briefly below.

Average True Range (ATR) is an exceptionally useful indicator that usually resides either vertically above or below the bar/candle price chart. ATR is an average measure of recent volatility. It is calculated as a moving average of a given past period of price ranges. When the ATR has a high reading, recent volatility has been high. When a low reading is given, recent volatility has been low. ATR is used by technical currency traders to determine the recent level of trading activity and volatility for a given currency pair. ATR can also be used for setting logical stop losses and price targets based on volatility, among other uses.

The Average Directional Index (ADX) also resides either vertically above or below the bar/candle price chart. ADX measures the strength of the current trend, not the direction of the trend. Strong trends, whether up or down, have high ADX readings, while nontrending, ranging markets have low ADX readings. ADX is an important indicator that can help a foreign exchange trader determine whether to use trend-trading techniques or range-trading techniques.

Bollinger Bands are overlaid directly on the price bars/candles. They consist of a simple moving average (SMA) with two additional lines, one that is a certain number of standard deviations above the SMA and the other that is the same number of standard deviations below the SMA. By default, Bollinger Bands are usually set at a 20-period SMA with 2 standard deviations above and below the moving average. But these settings can be readily changed to suit

EXHIBIT 3.19

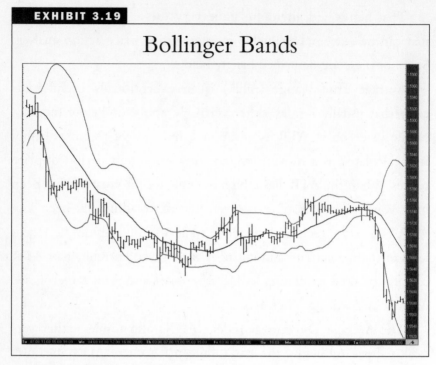

Bollinger Bands

Source: FX Solutions – FX AccuCharts

the trading environment. The primary purpose of the Bollinger Bands indicator is to measure a currency pair's volatility around the mean. The Bands are often used to give indications of impending volatility increases (when the bands tighten). They can also be used to provide indications of overbought or oversold market conditions. See Exhibit 3.19.

The Parabolic Stop-And-Reverse (SAR) is an indicator that excels at providing a sensible trailing stop and reverse methodology. Trailing stops are useful elements of an overall stop loss strategy, and will be discussed further in the section of Chapter 6 that covers risk management. The Parabolic SAR dots follow price such that if a

TIPS AND TECHNIQUES

The Bollinger Squeeze

There are almost as many different ways to interpret Bollinger Bands as there are traders using them to make trading decisions. But according to John Bollinger, CFA, CMT, famed originator of the Bands that bear his name, "The Squeeze" is perhaps the most popular topic related to this powerful indicator. Bollinger is the founder and president of Bollinger Capital Management and BollingerBands.com, and his work has long been renowned among professional traders and investors alike.

His book, *Bollinger on Bollinger Bands*, describes The Squeeze in considerable detail. He writes, "Bollinger Bands are driven by volatility, and The Squeeze is a pure reflection of that volatility. When volatility falls to historically low levels, The Squeeze is on."

He proceeds to write, "Time and again, we see The Squeeze in action. A consolidation begins. The resulting trading range narrows dramatically. The Bollinger Bands begin to tighten around the price structure. The stage is set."

The well-documented theory behind The Squeeze is that periods of high volatility generally follow periods of low volatility. When the Bollinger Bands narrow dramatically, volatility is drastically decreased. The subsequent expectation, then, is for price to breakout violently in either direction. This can potentially be a very tradable event.

But Bollinger goes on to caution, "Traders beware! There is a trick to The Squeeze, an odd turning of the wheel that you need to be aware of, the head fake. Often as the end of a Squeeze nears, price will stage a short fake-out move, and then abruptly turn and surge in the direction of the emerging trend."

If proper caution is exercised to control the risk inherent in the common "fake-out" moves, The Squeeze can be an effective tool in any forex trader's repertoire.

dot is below the price bar, the trade should be long with a dynamic stop loss at the dot. Conversely, if the dot is above the price bar, the trade should be short with a dynamic stop loss at the dot. Like many other indicators, the Parabolic SAR can be prone to vicious whipsaws where the trading signals result in a string of losses due to a lack of trend. But the fact that this indicator stresses a logical use of the trailing stop-loss concept makes it a valuable tool for the technical trader.

Besides the indicators described above, there is another special class of indicators, called oscillators, that fulfills an important role. Many of the oscillators, like Momentum and RSI, are very similar in formula and function. So they will not all be discussed here. Instead, only the most important and unique oscillators that are most applicable to foreign exchange trading will be covered. Oscillators excel at providing indications of overbought or oversold status during ranging markets. When an oscillator reading is above a certain overbought threshold during a trading range, it hints that upward momentum may soon be exhausted, and that an impending downward turn may occur. Conversely, when an oscillator reading is below a certain oversold threshold during a trading range, it hints that downward momentum may soon be exhausted, and that an impending upward turn may occur.

As will be seen in Chapter 5, oscillators also excel at providing divergence signals, among other functions. Divergence can provide important clues as to the possible direction of future momentum.

The Moving Average Convergence Divergence (MACD) is among the most popular indicators/oscillators ever invented. Many traders use MACD as their sole confirming oscillator. Some traders

EXHIBIT 3.20

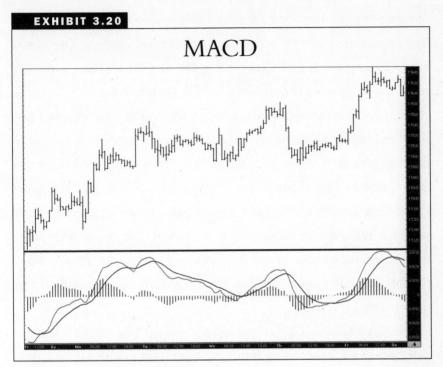

MACD

Source: FX Solutions — FX AccuCharts

also take trading signals exclusively from MACD. This multifaceted indicator acts as a sign of trend momentum by representing the relationship between two moving averages. MACD can be traded by taking signals from crossovers of the two lines, crosses above and below the zero line, and price-oscillator divergence, among other uses. See Exhibit 3.20.

Relative Strength Index (RSI) is another popular oscillator that provides a measure of price momentum. RSI is a classic oscillator that excels at giving overbought and oversold signals in ranging markets. Its usefulness, like most other oscillators, tends to diminish considerably during trending markets. RSI may also be used for divergence purposes. One of its primary usages is as a trade confirmation tool that identifies overbought/oversold markets. The mathematical formula for RSI compares the magnitude of a currency pair's recent gains to the magnitude of its recent losses.

The Stochastics oscillators come in several different flavors—fast, slow, and full. Whichever variety is chosen, the purpose is similar to other oscillators—identify overbought/oversold and provide divergence signals. The mathematical formula for Stochastics compares the currency pair's closing price to its price range over a set period of time. Because Stochastics has two lines as opposed to RSI's one line, Stochastics can give off an additional signal that results when the %K line crosses the %D line. Slow Stochastics is a smoothed version of Fast Stochastics.

Rate of Change (ROC) is a very simple and classic oscillator that provides a basic momentum measure. The mathematical calculation for this oscillator measures the percent change from the price a given number of periods ago to the current price. Besides showing divergence and overbought/oversold, ROC can also provide signals when the oscillator goes above and below the zero line.

The Commodity Channel Index (CCI) is an important but misnamed oscillator. Just as comfortable in the equities and foreign exchange worlds as it is in the futures/commodities arena, CCI has proven itself to be a popular oscillator for currency trading. Originally intended to identify cycles in the commodities markets, CCI has grown to become a highly valued tool in foreign exchange trading. Although CCI adherents have invented many different methods of analyzing this oscillator, its popular usage remains similar to the other oscillators—to identify divergences, as well as to point out overbought/oversold areas in the attempts to forecast price reversals at extremes.

The indicators and oscillators described in this section make up just a fraction of the technical studies available on most charting platforms. Some of these platforms offer hundreds of different studies. But the ones just mentioned comprise some of the most essential and useful indicators/oscillators available, and therefore merit the most extensive consideration.

Pointing the Way with Pivot Points

The pivot point method of trading has made its way to the foreign exchange markets from its use in futures and equities trading. Pivot points are support and resistance levels derived mathematically from the previous day's key data points. To calculate the main pivot point, for example, a trader would take the average of the previous day's high, low, and close. Then, four additional pivot points (named S1, S2, R1, and R2, where S=Support and R=Resistance) are calculated based on the central pivot point. Traders often add even more pivot points beyond the basic four plus the central pivot, but these are considered the most common and essential levels. See Exhibit 3.21.

The idea behind pivot points is that they can act as key support and resistance levels, where price may turn as in a retracement or correction. Many analysts believe that like some other technical tools, pivot points are a self-fulfilling prophecy. In other words, they work only because enough traders believe in them and trade off of them that there is bound to be some significant price activity at those levels. This self-fulfilling prophecy concept can also be

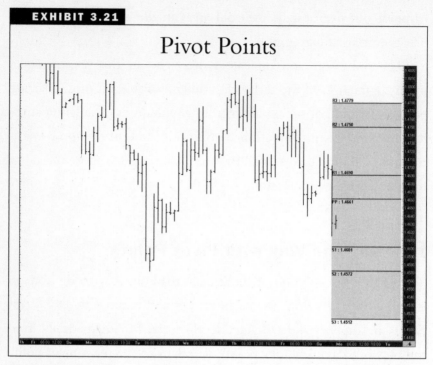

EXHIBIT 3.21

Pivot Points

Source: FX Solutions – FX AccuCharts

extended to trendlines, horizontal support/resistance lines, Fibonacci retracements, and other technical tools. The basics of trading with pivot points will be touched upon in Chapter 5.

Fibonacci's Magic Numbers

There is a long and interesting story behind Fibonacci numbers that is beyond the scope of this book. It should suffice to say that Leonardo Fibonacci was a 13th century Italian mathematician who calculated a sequence of numbers that ultimately led to the discovery of the golden ratio—1.618. This ratio, and its inverse of 0.618,

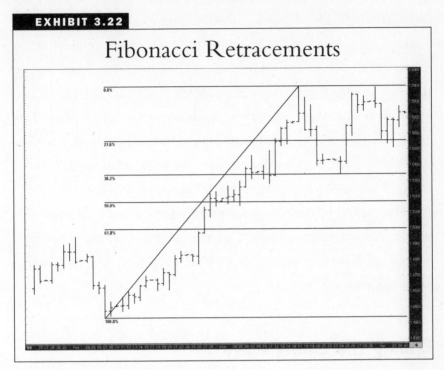

EXHIBIT 3.22

Fibonacci Retracements

Source: FX Solutions – FX AccuCharts

are purported to occur throughout science, nature, and art. Even a snail's shell is said to follow the laws of the golden ratio.

Because of the seemingly universal significance of this ratio, traders long ago began applying it to trading the financial markets. Today, technical analysts have many tools that are derived from the Golden Ratio and Fibonacci's work. The most important and popular of these is the Fibonacci Retracement tool. See Exhibit 3.22.

Drawn on a chart from a low price extreme to a high one, or vice versa, Fibonacci retracements help outline key support and resistance levels on retracements from the primary price move. For example, it should be expected that within an uptrend, price will retrace at some point. When it does, Fibonacci theory suggests that price will likely retrace a magnitude of 38.2%, 50%, or 61.8% of the original move. These are the most significant levels according to Fibonacci trading theory. Other important retracement levels include 23.6%, 76.4%, and 100%. Knowing where all of these levels occur on a given price chart can be instrumental in finding out where traders may be paying particular attention. As such, Fibonacci levels can be considered, to some extent, a self-fulfilling prophecy much like the pivot points.

The various Fibonacci tools, especially retracements, are extremely popular with foreign exchange traders. More information on how traders use Fibonacci principles to trade currencies will be touched upon in Chapter 5.

Riding the Elliott Wave

Related to Fibonacci methodology, Elliott Wave Theory is named after Ralph Nelson Elliott, who asserted that price movement is predictable and can be classified into a series of identifiable waves. The basic wave structure is a series of five waves comprising the primary trend movement with three waves comprising the corrective movement. Several rules and guidelines accompany this basic structure that makes Elliott Wave Theory a complete philosophy of trading. See Exhibit 3.23.

This trading philosophy is immensely popular with countless global adherents. Included among these adherents are some of the most competent traders and analysts in the world. Although some detractors may deem Elliott Wave analysis as too subjective to be consistently effective, the fact that scores of successful traders have long

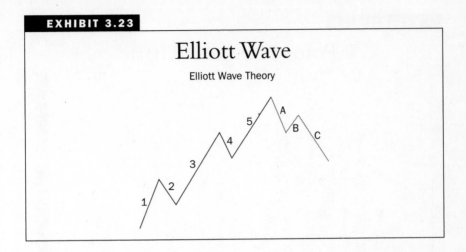

EXHIBIT 3.23

Elliott Wave

Elliott Wave Theory

abided by the tenets of this theory makes this a trading methodology that should not be ignored by foreign exchange traders. The Elliott Wave trading methodology will be described further in Chapter 5.

Getting to the Point & Figure

Point & figure (p&f) charting is an older, but still popular, form of technical analysis that constitutes an entire trading methodology unto itself. Some may characterize p&f charting as trading based upon pure price action. This is because only price, which is undeniably the most important aspect of technical analysis, is customarily included on this type of chart (in the form of Xs and Os). Other data that can readily be found on bar and candlestick charts, like time and period opens/closes, are generally excluded on p&f charts. This leaves only the uncluttered purity of price action. See Exhibit 3.24 for a typical forex point & figure chart.

The primary advantage of using p&f charting methodology over other types of charts (like bars and candlesticks) lies in the clearer

EXHIBIT 3.24

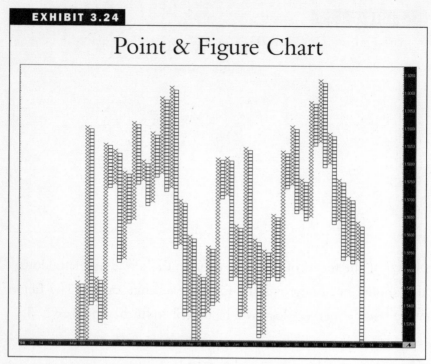

Point & Figure Chart

Source: FX Solutions – FX AccuCharts

and more simplified representation of trend, support/resistance, and breakouts. Generally, much of the up-and-down price "noise" that is so common in the foreign exchange markets is filtered out by p&f charts, leaving just the clarity of trend movement and direction. As will be described in Chapter 5, point & figure charting consists primarily of watching for price level breakouts.

Chapter Summary

Most foreign exchange traders use at least some form of technical analysis in their currency trading. The many tools of technical analysis begin with the basic chart, of which there are a couple of primary types.

Bar charts and candlestick charts are, by far, the most prevalent types of charts. From there, we move onto charting timeframes, of which there are many. Extremely short-term traders may use minute charts (where each bar/candlestick is worth a minute of price action), while longer-term traders may use hourly, daily, or weekly charts, among a myriad of other timeframes.

The real essentials of technical analysis lie partly in the twin phenomena of support and resistance, where price seems to be attracted to and repelled by these oft-visited levels. These levels are usually denoted with horizontal lines across the chart. Going a step further, trend lines and trend channels are sloped lines that point out dynamic support and resistance with respect to a directional trend. Moving averages also excel at outlining the general trend, as well as showing dynamic support and resistance levels.

Patterns are very common on currency charts. There are several different types of patterns that are prevalent. Japanese candlestick patterns that consist of single or multiple candles are, by definition, found only on candlestick charts. These include dojis, hammers, engulfing patterns, and so on. Larger, Western-style patterns like triangles, head-and-shoulders, flags, and pennants can be found on both bar and candlestick charts. All of these patterns paint a revealing picture to the experienced technical analyst.

Chart indicators also reveal information to technical traders. This information is primarily in the form of momentum readings and overbought/oversold levels. Mostly used to confirm trading signals from other technical analysis tools, indicators and oscillators are usually either overlaid right on top of the price bars/candlesticks, or separated in an area vertically above or below price.

Some other specialized technical analysis methods have also gained many adherents in the trading world. Often, comprehensive trading strategies have evolved around these techniques. These include pivot points, Fibonacci, and Elliott Wave, among others. Entire books can and have been written about each of these topics. It is in the best interests of every well-rounded foreign exchange trader to have at least a passing familiarity with these useful analytical methods.

Finally, although point & figure charts will perhaps never be able to surpass the widespread use of bar and candlestick charts, all serious technical analysts should be familiar with this granddaddy of charting types. Analysis on point & figure charts is significantly different from analysis performed on bar or candlestick charts. But the unique insights provided by point & figure charts, especially with respect to trend, support/resistance, and breakouts, can be extremely valuable to technical traders in the foreign exchange markets.

CHAPTER 4

Fundamental Analysis—What Drives the Foreign Exchange Markets

After reading this chapter, you will be able to:

- Recognize what really makes the foreign exchange markets move, and how best to take advantage of this knowledge.

- Appreciate how interest rates, inflation, economic growth, and other fundamental factors contribute to currency valuation.

- Identify the economic indicators that are essential for successful foreign exchange traders to know and understand.

- Apply the fundamental concepts of carry trading and news trading to your own market strategies.

Introduction to Fundamental Analysis—Basic Economics

Like technical analysis, fundamental analysis is another major aspect of financial analysis used for trading the foreign exchange markets. Whereas technical analysis is concerned primarily with interpreting price action, fundamental analysis concentrates on such topics as economic data, government policy, sociopolitical conditions, global news, and the business cycle. These topics include an array of different variables, most notable of which include macroeconomic factors like interest rates, inflation, central bank policy, economic growth, housing, employment, industrial and commercial production, and the list goes on and on.

Whereas technical analysis excels at providing logical trade entries and exits, fundamental analysis can provide a framework for formulating a longer-term opinion on the global currency markets. Because of this, with the notable exception of news trading and carry trading (which will both be discussed later in this chapter and in Chapter 5), there is a lack of practical and concrete trading methodologies for retail forex traders that utilize fundamental analysis exclusively. In other words, an individual foreign exchange trader could certainly try to place trades based solely on a fundamental understanding of economic and political factors. But in doing so, the placement of trade entries and exits could be considered essentially an arbitrary act without the precise entry/exit methods of technical analysis.

That being said, however, fundamental analysis is an extremely vital and indispensable aspect of successful foreign exchange trading. Fundamental factors, or the market's perceptions of these factors, are essentially what make the currency markets move.

Technicals without the fundamentals makes for just as incomplete a trader as fundamentals alone. These two aspects of foreign exchange market analysis complement each other extremely well, and are two of the key ingredients to approaching foreign exchange trading in an intelligent, well-rounded manner. Even those technical purists who refuse to heed fundamental information, insisting that all of this information is already reflected in the price charts, would be well served to pay attention at least to how central bank policy, economic data announcements, and major sociopolitical events may affect price.

While all of these concepts are integral elements of the fundamental approach, the main crux of fundamental analysis clearly lies in the framework of basic economics. Currencies appreciate and depreciate in value because of simple economic supply and demand factors. If there is a progressively higher demand for and/or lower supply of a certain country's currency, its value should increase. Conversely, if there is a progressively lower demand for and/or higher supply of a currency, its value should decrease. It is the foreign exchange speculator's job to determine in which direction the shifting of supply and demand is most likely to occur.

There are many factors that can contribute to this shifting of supply/demand for the world's currencies. One of the most important of these factors is interest rates, which will be discussed next.

A Healthy Interest in Global Bank Rates

Global interest rates are one of the primary drivers of currency exchange rates. Generally speaking, when all other variables are kept equal, rising interest rates (central bank tightening) have a tendency to contribute to an appreciation in a currency. This is because higher-yielding currencies attract more demand from large institutional investors, who are consistently in search of ways to earn more on their money. If, on the other hand, there is a lowering of interest rates (central bank easing), the tendency is towards a depreciation of the currency. This is due to decreasing demand by the institutional investors, who generally tend to move their money away from lower-yielding assets. Although this may constitute a simplistic assumption regarding international capital flows, as so many other factors contribute to exchange rate movement, interest rates generally tend to exert their influence in this manner.

It should be kept in mind, from a foreign exchange trading perspective, that the appreciation or depreciation in an exchange rate is less a product of the absolute value of the interest rate than the direction of change in the interest rate. In other words, although the current interest rate for a country's currency is important in helping the market to determine its exchange value, the direction of interest rate change is even more important. Just because a currency carries a high-yield does not ensure an appreciation in the exchange rate. But if the currency's central bank continues to raise interest rates and indicates an intention to keep doing so, this can have a considerable impact on appreciation in the currency.

Changes in interest rates are initiated by central bank policy. In the United States, this central bank is the Federal Reserve (informally called the "Fed"). Other major central banks include the European Central Bank (ECB), the Bank of England (BOE), the Bank of Japan (BOJ), the Bank of Canada (BOC), and the Reserve Bank of Australia (RBA). These institutions make decisions that help determine the direction of interest rates.

In adjusting interest rates, central banks seek to achieve a delicate balance between attaining a significant level of economic growth while staving off excessive inflation. A certain controlled level of inflation is necessary for economic growth, as a country without inflation is a sign of a stagnant economy. At the same time, however, excessive inflation can be enormously disadvantageous to an economy and its consumers. Therefore, each central bank must take both goals of economic growth and inflation control into serious consideration when setting monetary policy.

In view of these goals, there are a couple of primary reasons why a central bank would seek to change interest rates. These are by no means the only reasons, but they are usually among the most compelling ones for central banks. Generally speaking, central banks will look to increase interest rates (tighten) in order to help stave off excessive inflation. Conversely, central banks will look to decrease interest rates (ease) in order to help stimulate economic growth. Either way, central banks have the power to impact the foreign exchange markets enormously by making changes in interest rate policy.

Often, an actual change in rate policy is not even needed to affect a currency's value. Merely a comment hinting at potential policy intention within a speech by the Fed chairman, for example, is often sufficient to trigger drastic price moves. This highlights the fact that it is not as much the actual fundamentals that move currency exchange rates. Rather, it is more the traders' collective perceptions and expectations of the fundamentals that truly drive these markets.

Carried Away with Trading

Within the context of trading foreign exchange based on fundamental factors, one of the primary trading/investment models utilized both by institutional and retail traders is the carry trade. Further information on carry trading will be discussed in Chapter 5, but the general concept will be described here.

The carry trade is primarily a longer-term fundamental investment strategy used by foreign exchange participants to exploit interest rate differentials between currencies. Used in conjunction with the high leverage ratios commonly offered in foreign exchange trading, this strategy can produce exceptionally magnified returns while also carrying a significant degree of risk.

The basic idea behind carry trading is to buy a currency with a high interest rate while simultaneously selling another currency with a low interest rate. The net effect is that the trader earns a positive yield based on the differential between the two interest rates.

For example, suppose a foreign exchange trader buys AUD/JPY, which is a frequently carry-traded pair due to the traditionally wide interest rate differential between the Australian dollar and the Japanese yen. Buying, or being long, the AUD/JPY is the same as buying AUD while simultaneously selling JPY. Another way to look at a long position in AUD/JPY is the concept of borrowing the yen (low interest rate) in order to buy the aussie (high interest rate). Either way it is viewed, the result is the same—the trader earns the high rate while paying the low rate, or the trader earns the differential between the rates (minus the inevitable interest rate spread).

If trading with one of the major retail foreign exchange bro-kers, the carry trader earns daily interest profits for all open posi-tions whose interest rate differential is positive, as in the case of a long position in AUD/JPY. Based on the size of the trader's open position and the amount of leverage used, this positive yield is con-verted into a monetary amount that is actually paid directly into the trader's account each day when the foreign exchange broker "rolls over" open positions.

As mentioned earlier, because of the highly leveraged nature of foreign exchange trading, this amount can be substantial. But it should be kept in mind that interest rates can also work against trad-ers in an equally substantial manner if positions that carry a negative differential are kept open. To use AUD/JPY once again as an exam-ple, it could get very expensive from an interest rate perspective to hold a short position open in this pair. Short AUD/JPY is the same as being short aussie (high interest rate) while simultaneously being long yen (low interest rate), or borrowing at the high interest rate to buy at the low interest rate. The net result in terms of the rate differ-ential is negative, which means the trader is required to pay a daily interest amount for the open position based on the negative differ-ential, the size of the trade, and the amount of leverage used.

It is therefore imperative that foreign exchange traders pay close attention to interest rate differentials on all trades initiated, espe-cially those that will likely remain as open positions for more than a day. Whether positive or negative, interest rate differentials can have an extremely significant impact on the daily balance in a foreign exchange trading account. More on how traders may take advantage of the positive interest rate differentials so eagerly sought-after by carry traders (while mitigating the inherent exchange rate risks) will be discussed in Chapter 5.

Indication of Things to Come—Economic Indicators

Aside from interest rates and central bank policy, one of the most vitally important fundamental factors to foreign exchange traders is economic data. Even technical traders who eschew the use of fundamental analysis should at least know when data are being released (by referring to any online economic data calendar), but should preferably go even a step further by understanding the ramifications of each release. Economic data and news announcements help drive both short-term and long-term movements in currency exchange rates, so it behooves all foreign exchange traders to know at least what every major data point means, if not the underlying nuances of each.

On the opposite extreme from the technical-trading purists, a whole legion of short-term foreign exchange traders actually live and die by fundamental data and news announcements. During news time, many of these traders simply sit at their computers—trigger finger on the buy/sell button and live news feed blasting—waiting for economic data to be released publicly so a trade can be entered. In order to profit with a few pips, news traders who trade foreign exchange in this manner must be quick to make a split-second assessment of the news or data, and then place a corresponding trade within milliseconds. The trade must then be closed for either a profit or a loss, often only seconds after the trade was entered. This is not an easy method of trading, and it most certainly is not for everyone. But many of those who can make it work claim to reap consistent success with this method. Further details on news trading will be discussed later in this chapter and in Chapter 5.

When economic data are released, currency pairs relating to the specific release often react in extreme ways. For news traders, the best possible reaction is for price to initiate a one-way run without looking back. Often, however, extreme nondirectional volatility is the order of the day, where price just seems to jump up and down, whipsawing every position in sight. This is every foreign exchange trader's nightmare. In any event, the major, market-moving economic data indicators need to be identified and studied in order for a trader to have any chance of trading currencies successfully during and after data releases.

Following are the key economic indicators relevant to the U.S. dollar. These indicators constitute the major economic data reports released periodically to the public by government agencies and private entities. Of course, there are many other indicators that come out every day affecting the many non-U.S. currencies. But since the vast majority of trading volume in the foreign exchange markets is centered primarily on U.S. dollar-based currency pairs (more than 90%), the following is an excellent representative sampling of the fundamental indicators that help drive the global currency markets. Within this list, the relative importance and market-moving potential of each indicator may change from month-to-month and year-to-year, so the indicators are listed in no particular order:

- Gross Domestic Product (GDP)—GDP is perhaps the most consistently followed and studied economic indicator for foreign exchange traders. This is because it is virtually an all-encompassing measure of economic growth and output. Released quarterly and quoted on an annualized basis, the GDP is the total market value of all goods and services produced by the economy within a given period of time. Real GDP, which is GDP adjusted for inflation, takes into account price level changes, and so is considered a more accurate reflection of production than the original GDP percentage. When the real GDP report is released on a quarterly basis, foreign exchange markets often move in a substantial manner. This is due to the fact that real GDP is perhaps the best single assessment of an economy's health available to market participants. Therefore, if there is one economic indicator that all foreign exchange traders should be aware of, it is the real GDP statistic.

- Employment situation—The Employment Situation Report is put out monthly by the Bureau of Labor Statistics, and includes two vitally important surveys that summarize the nation's labor situation: the Household Survey, and the Establishment Survey. Within these surveys are some figures that have been known in the past several years to move the foreign exchange markets significantly. Most notable of these figures is the Non-Farm Payrolls (NFP) data (within the Establishment Survey), which has been one of the most anticipated and traded benchmark statistics by foreign exchange traders in recent years. At the height of its popularity, legions of foreign exchange traders have been known to sit eagerly at their trading stations on the first Friday of every month, waiting nervously for the NFP numbers to be released. Like these NFP numbers, the unemployment rate data (within the Household Survey) also constitutes a major, market-moving statistic.

- Retail sales—Another very important economic indicator, the monthly Retail sales report releases data for the previous month on the value of merchandise sold to end consumers by a representative sampling of retailers. Retail sales data includes the total retail sales in dollars, with the percentage change from the prior month. It also includes the total retail sales excluding automobile sales ("ex-autos"). This is because auto sales tend to skew the total sales figure in a way that would render it somewhat misleading. Retail sales data provides traders with a broad measure of sales activity, and therefore, an accurate reflection of the economy's health as a whole. It can also give strong indications of potential inflation, interest rate change, and possibly even recession. Therefore, this economic indicator is one that foreign exchange traders should pay special attention to.

- Consumer Price Index (CPI)—Because the monthly CPI is a benchmark inflation indicator, it is one of the most anticipated releases by the foreign exchange trading community. The CPI takes a basket of common, daily-use consumer products and compares price levels from previous years. Two metrics comprise the CPI statistics—Core CPI (minus food and energy) and chain-weighted CPI. Core CPI is more anticipated by traders than chain-weighted CPI. Because CPI is probably the best set of statistics for indicating inflation, it can be effective in giving hints as to future potential interest rate changes by the Fed. For this reason alone, CPI is extremely worth watching by foreign exchange traders.

- Producer Price Index (PPI)—From a foreign exchange trading perspective, the primary role of the monthly PPI, which is released before the CPI every month, is essentially as a predictor of the all-important CPI inflation-indicator. Whereas the CPI is an index of consumer prices, the PPI is an index of producer, or wholesale, prices. Since consumer prices and producer prices are closely interrelated, the PPI and CPI are generally close reflections of each other. Within the PPI, core PPI (minus food and energy) is the most followed statistic. Because inflation and interest rates are so important to the value of the U.S. dollar—and the CPI is perhaps the most accurate indicator of inflation available—the PPI is also an important economic indicator because it is, in turn, an accurate predictor of the CPI.

- Durable goods—The Durable Goods Report is a monthly report that provides data on new orders placed with domestic manufacturers for delivery of durable goods. These are defined as factory hard goods with a useful life of at least three years, and generally include higher-priced products such as automobiles, appliances, industrial machinery, computers, and the like. The Durable Goods Report is one of the economic indicators that paint a picture of the U.S. manufacturing sector, which is a vital aspect of the economy. Therefore, the report also reflects general business demand and confidence within the entire economy. For these reasons, this indicator can certainly move the currency markets, especially if the numbers deviate significantly from the expected consensus numbers (more on consensus will be discussed later in this chapter).

- Industrial production—The Industrial Production Report is a monthly measure of the percentage change in manufacturing and factory production. Like the Durable Goods Report, the Industrial Production Report is important because it provides information on the vital manufacturing sector. Significant changes in this sector can signal changes in the entire economy, including economic growth, inflation, and recession. Therefore, this economic indicator contains useful data for the foreign exchange trader.

- Purchasing Managers Index (PMI)—The Institute for Supply Management (ISM), a nonprofit group, maintains the PMI and issues monthly releases based upon this index. The PMI is a composite index of the manufacturing situation that includes: new orders, production level, employment, supplier delivery times, and inventories. Data for this index, which is essentially a sentiment indicator for the national manufacturing sector, are obtained through surveys of purchasing managers. Like the Durable Goods Report and the Industrial Production Report, PMI releases are important to the foreign exchange market because they provide a good measure of the manufacturing sector, which is an integral component of U.S. economic health.

- Employment Cost Index (ECI)—The ECI is a quarterly report released by the Bureau of Labor Statistics (BLS). This report measures changes in payroll compensation costs for nonfarm industries, as well as state and local governments (but excludes federal government). Like the CPI, the ECI is used mainly for its role as an inflation indicator. Because of this, and the fact that the Fed uses it to help decide monetary policy, the ECI is a useful economic indicator for foreign exchange traders to watch.

- Housing starts/existing home sales—Together, Housing Starts (New Residential Construction Report) and the Existing Home Sales Report provide a solid picture of the U.S. housing situation. Housing starts is issued monthly by the U.S. Census Bureau. Through surveys of homebuilders, it collects data primarily with regard to the percentage change in housing starts (new homes on which construction of the foundation has begun) and building permits. Housing starts is often used as an indicator of where the economy falls within the current business cycle. The Existing Home Sales Report, on the other hand, is a monthly release by the National Association of Realtors that measures the number of existing homes that were closed on (sold) in the previous month, along with average sales prices. Like Housing Starts, the Existing Home Sales Report also provides business cycle indications. When taken as a whole, these two reports accurately reflect the state of the U.S. housing market. This, in turn, can provide strong guidance for the U.S. dollar during times when the housing situation is negatively affecting the entire economy.

- Trade balance—The monthly Trade Balance Report is important to foreign exchange traders because it has become an indicator of U.S. economic health, as well as U.S. economic standing in relation to foreign economies. The nominal trade deficit data, which represents the difference in monetary value between exports and imports, is probably the most watched and anticipated aspect of the Trade Balance Report. Data from this report can have an impact on the foreign exchange markets in several ways. One of these ways has to do with changing supply and demand for a currency (in this case, the U.S. dollar). If there is a decreasing U.S. trade deficit, countries importing more U.S. products must convert their funds to U.S. dollars, thereby increasing the general demand for dollars and making the dollar appreciate. If, on the other hand, there is an increasing U.S. trade deficit, with the U.S. buying more foreign goods, this will necessitate the selling of dollars and buying of more foreign currencies to pay for those foreign goods. This generally results in a greater supply of dollars, and therefore potential dollar depreciation. The Trade Balance Report can certainly move the foreign exchange markets when released, but especially if the numbers show a large change from the previous period, or if they deviate considerably from consensus estimates.

• Personal income and outlays—The Personal Income and Outlays Report is a monthly release by the Bureau of Economic Analysis (BEA). Personal income is the amount of income received by individuals from all sources, especially wages and salaries. Personal outlays consist primarily of consumer purchases of goods and services. Components of this report include Real Personal Income (income per capita adjusted for inflation), Disposable Personal Income (income less tax payments), Personal Savings Rate (Disposable Personal Income less personal outlays), and Personal Consumption Expenditures (PCE). This last component, the PCE Index, provides a measure of how much individuals are spending, including on consumer goods and even credit card interest. Personal income data are important to foreign exchange traders because it is a strong indicator of future demand, and it acts as a barometer for the consumer sector. In terms of personal outlays, or consumption, the PCE Index has become one of the key indicators of inflation, as well as a major component of GDP. For these reasons, foreign exchange traders would be remiss to ignore the information contained in the Personal Income and Outlays Report.

- Federal Open Market Committee (FOMC) rate decisions— As is evident from earlier in this chapter, interest rates are a major determinant of currency value. An FOMC rate decision is not as much of an economic data indicator as the others described in this section. Rather, it is a market-moving announcement resulting from an all-important meeting on interest rates, inflation, and the economy by the top Fed board members and bank presidents in the country. The FOMC, which currently has eight regularly scheduled meetings per year, is a major element of the Federal Reserve System, and it serves as the primary director of U.S. monetary policy. The central component of this policy is the setting of target levels for the Fed Funds rate, which is the interest rate that banks charge each other on overnight loans. Needless to say, because of the FOMC's influence on interest rates, its decisions can have an enormous impact on the foreign exchange markets. Especially when there is a large change or unexpected departure from consensus, FOMC rate decisions can immediately move the currency markets in an extreme manner.

Joseph Trevisani

With all of the media news and noise that may affect the foreign exchange markets, it can be extremely tricky to decipher which pieces of information actually drive currency prices in a major way. An expert in fundamental analysis, Joseph Trevisani—Chief Market Analyst at FX Solutions (FXSolutions.com)—serves as an invaluable guide for separating the truly important information from the not-so-important. With around two decades of experience as an institutional currency trader and trading desk manager at large global banks, Trevisani appears regularly on financial news channels and is quoted frequently by the major financial press.

In an interview with the author, Trevisani states:

"Central bank interest rates have a higher positive correlation with the value of a country's currency than any other factor. The country with the higher rate will generally have the more valuable currency. If British rates are higher than American rates they will support the value of the pound against the dollar, and vice versa. Banks in countries with a rate advantage both pay more on deposits and attract more funds to earn the higher rate. But for the currency markets the composition of the central bank rate cycle is just as important as the comparison between current rates. Central banks rarely make one rate adjustment. Rates tend to move in cycles, a series of rate cuts or increases over time, as the central bank responds to changing economic conditions and attempts to anticipate future conditions. It is the change in these cycles, or the advent of a new cycle, that drives currency markets. When a central bank recalibrates its economic view, the currency markets tend to build-in a large portion of the prospective rate cycle almost immediately. Trading rates will adjust quickly to the new view. Central banks play different roles within their respective economies, determined both by conception and tradition. The European Central Bank has a specific mandate to protect against inflation—economic growth is secondary. The American Federal Reserve's role is to promote economic growth and jobs, as well as to watch against inflation. Almost all central banks have responsibility for the functioning of the national financial system, though the degree varies. A central bank's rate policy is primarily determined by domestic economic circumstance and not by a desire or a need to affect the value of its currency on the international stage.

The value of a nation's currency is also directly affected by the comparative strength and weakness of a country's economy in relation to those of its trading partners. The stronger economy, that with the higher GDP growth, lower inflation, greater productivity, political stability and a host of other factors will, over time, have the stronger currency. It is these fundamental factors, in conjunction with central bank interest rate cycles, which produce the long-lasting price trends typical of the currency markets. Some factors that affect a country's economic status reflect the choices of the political system. The balance between social welfare and individual competition is one example—the openness of an economy to foreign trade and capital is another. Other economic factors such as labor mobility, entrepreneurship, and savings rates are part of the social and cultural makeup of the nation. And yet others, like oil or mineral deposits, stem from a nation's geographic or resource endowment. All of these factors, and many more, are monitored, assessed and judged for their effect on economic growth and development. A change in one factor or several can affect the productivity capacity of an economy, alter its competitiveness against its trading partners, and change the relative value of its currency.

Exchange rates tend to focus on one aspect of a currency—its use as a medium of exchange. The U.S. economy is currently 22% of world GDP; it was once 50%. Modern industrial capitalism is spreading to new and ever-larger sections of the world. Since World War II the U.S. percentage of the world economy has steadily diminished as other national economies have grown at faster rates. Over time that reduction has decreased the demand for the dollar as an agent of exchange. But currencies also act as a long term store of value. Any foreign investor in a country is also an investor in that country's currency. When a central bank or private entity buys United States Treasury Bonds or American stocks, it does so with dollars, creating demand for the U.S. currency. Until the creation of the euro there was no alternative to the dollar as a store of value. No other country could match the economic, technological and political power of the United States, and these qualities made it a favorite investment destination. The demand for the dollar as a store of value created by investment flow added greatly to its demand in the currency markets."

No News Is Bad News for News Traders

With economic news and data coming out of the United States and other countries on an ongoing basis, foreign exchange traders who truly strive to be successful, regardless of whether they are primarily technical or fundamental strategists, must necessarily be vigilant of scheduled economic releases and current events. Fundamental forces affect currency prices too thoroughly to ignore. But when traders concentrate all of their attention on news and economic data to the exclusion of other factors, this is called news trading.

As mentioned earlier in this chapter, news trading can be difficult for a number of reasons. One notable difficulty is the speed that is required to place trades at the right time in order to take advantage of the best price moves on a data release. These moves can take place during or only milliseconds after the release, and traders need to compete with countless other individuals and institutions that are placing trades at the same time.

In addition, obtaining the news earlier than others is virtually impossible for the average individual trader. Most traders do not have access to the almost instantaneous news feeds that are necessary for trading the news effectively. Any lag time in receiving data releases translates into potentially lost profits.

Furthermore, during and immediately after news releases are among the most volatile times for the currency markets. This means that it may be harder for trades to be filled by the broker as accurately as during quieter markets. This is due to the sheer speed of price movement as well as the price gaps that can occur in fast markets.

Besides the speed factor, another underlying difficulty with news trading involves the proper interpretation of the news. Economic data releases and other news announcements hold many nuances that can be difficult for the average foreign exchange trader to comprehend fully. Often, a new economic number comes out that should obviously make the dollar go up, but instead, the dollar plummets, or vice versa. This is where the concept of consensus comes in.

When a piece of news or data release comes out and the market does something intuitively different or opposite of what it should do, traders will say that the information was already "priced in" to the market. For example, if bad news for the dollar comes out but the dollar goes up anyway, it should mean that the market was already expecting bad news. Maybe the news that ultimately came out, though bad, was not as bad as traders had been expecting. When a market expecting horrible news receives only bad news, the relatively positive nature of the bad news will often make the market go up. In this example, the expectation of horrible news is called the consensus.

Foreign exchange traders who trade the news must pay attention not only to the actual numbers that are released, but also to the consensus, or what the economists and other experts are expecting. Then, trading can take place based on how far the actual numbers deviate from the consensus numbers. In this way, news trading is based almost entirely on relative values rather than absolute values. Often, news traders will determine their own trading threshold for the difference between actual data and consensus data, placing long or short trades only if the respective threshold is met or exceeded by the actual data.

One final point regarding economic indicators and trading the news lies in the economic data issuer's common practice of releasing revisions. For example, if Non-Farm Payrolls data are released on the first Friday in February describing employment figures for the month of January, what will sometimes happen is that those January numbers will be significantly revised when the new Non-Farm-Payrolls report comes out in March. If substantial enough, this March revision has the potential to move the foreign exchange markets even more than the original report released in February. Therefore, the prudent news trader must necessarily pay close attention not only to consensus and actual data figures, but also to the possibility of unexpected revisions.

As many fundamental news traders will attest, because of all the difficulties involved in trading the news, including those described here, it is definitely a very challenging style of trading. Those who take the time and trouble to overcome the obstacles, though, often find it a very rewarding one.

Chapter Summary

Fundamental analysis is essentially the study of why markets move, or, more specifically, what drives them to move. The primary drivers in foreign exchange, like that of other financial markets, are the basic economic concepts of supply and demand. If there is high demand for and/or low supply of a currency, its value should go up. Conversely, if there is low demand for and/or high supply of a currency, its value should go down.

In turn, supply and demand are driven primarily by traders' collective perceptions of fundamental factors. These factors include interest rates, central bank policy, economic growth, and inflation, among others. Changes in these factors can have profound effects on the currency markets.

In terms of interest rates and central bank policy, which are instrumental determinants of currency value, central banks will tend to increase rates (tighten) with the goal of controlling inflation. On the other hand, these banks will seek to decrease rates (ease) in order to help stimulate the economy. Generally speaking, the immediate effect of tightening tends toward an appreciation of the currency, while the immediate effect of easing tends toward a depreciation of the currency. These are only general tendencies—not rules—as many different factors combine to dictate currency exchange rates.

Also in the realm of interest rates, carry traders can earn interest income on the interest rate differential for the currency pair they are trading, provided the trade is in the direction of positive interest. For example, for a carry-traded pair like AUD/JPY (where AUD has a high interest rate and JPY has a low interest rate) a trader would earn a positive differential for holding a long AUD/JPY position, and would be charged as a result of a negative differential for holding a short AUD/JPY position.

Also important to the value of a currency, and what many short-term foreign exchange traders gravitate towards, are economic data indicators. These indicators are usually released on a monthly or quarterly basis by government agencies or private organizations, and they each provide a barometer reading for a certain sector or aspect of the economy. For example, GDP is used for assessing economic growth, CPI for providing indications of inflation, and the Non-Farm Payrolls report for evaluating the employment situation.

News traders in the foreign exchange markets seek to exploit these economic data releases by trading currencies based on how the actual data figures may deviate from the predetermined consensus figures. In this way, these traders are using the twin concepts of market expectation and surprise to dictate their trading. There are many difficulties involved in this type of trading, but those who are able to overcome the significant obstacles often find news trading to be a worthwhile pursuit.

Regardless of whether one is classified primarily as a technical analyst or a fundamental analyst, it is absolutely essential for any foreign exchange trader who wishes to have a reasonable chance at success to pay at least some attention to the fundamentals. The more a trader learns about fundamental market drivers, the better that trader will be prepared for the often unpredictable nature of the foreign exchange markets.

CHAPTER 5

Foreign Exchange Trading Methods and Strategies

After reading this chapter, you will be able to:

- Appreciate the many methods and strategies commonly used by experienced foreign exchange traders.

- Comprehend the logic and reasoning behind the most popular forex trading styles.

- Execute specific, high-probability strategies in a foreign exchange trading account.

- Understand the basics of backtesting and autotrading.

Rules to Trade By

Here is where all that has been learned thus far, especially with regard to basic trading mechanics and technical/fundamental analysis, can be combined to form cohesive trading methods and strategies with definitive rules to trade by. Knowledge of market analysis alone is simply not enough to trade foreign exchange effectively. In order to be successful, each trader must necessarily integrate the principles of market analysis into structured, workable trading processes that offer the best chances of consistent profitability. This is where trading methods and strategies come in.

When reading this chapter, keep in mind that the lines between each trading method/strategy/system/style can often be excessively blurred. For example, swing trading shares many similarities with range trading. The same may be said for position trading and long-term trend trading. Similarly, point & figure trading is sometimes considered breakout trading at its finest. The point is that each of these ways of tackling the foreign exchange market will have its own separate heading, but the overlap among them can be substantial. This is due to the fact that there are almost as many ways to trade currencies as there are traders in the financial markets, and each particular way of trading does not always fit precisely into one neat bucket. This chapter will provide an overview of some of the main methods of trading forex that have proven themselves over time, as well as some specifics regarding how to go about applying those methods.

It should also be noted here that none of these methods can be considered the "holy grail" of forex trading. In fact, there is no such thing as a holy grail in the trading world. No trading method or strategy could ever offer any trader a guaranteed promise of success and profitability. The closest thing that comes to anything resembling a holy grail would be a combination of several factors, including: broad trading experience, extensive market knowledge, sufficient risk capital, prudent money management, a good trading plan, and a first-rate trading strategy with a positive expectancy. To a degree, this book can help with the crucial aspects of knowledge, risk/money management, a trading plan, and a trading strategy. But obviously, experience and capital are entirely in the hands of each individual trader.

What the following trading methods and strategies will provide is a head start into the world of real, hands-on currency trading. Armed with the methods and strategies contained herein, as well as a free practice trading account from any online forex broker, prospective traders can immediately begin to explore the ways in which experienced traders approach the foreign exchange markets. It is highly recommended that traders practice any new method extensively on a demo practice account before attempting to apply it on a real money account. Again, successful trading is not just about a great trading strategy. If a trader is to be successful, that individual must necessarily synchronize many positive attributes in conjunction with a good method or strategy.

In no particular order, the foreign exchange trading styles, methods, and strategies to be discussed in this book will begin with three general approaches to forex trading in common use: position trading, swing trading, and day trading. Traders generally choose (or evolve into) an approach based on their personality, experience, and risk appetite, among other factors.

Position Trading—Settling in for the Long Term

As its label suggests, position trading is all about taking a directional market position and holding it for as long as the trade makes sense from a trend standpoint. This usually means that positions are held longer-term. In the fast-moving, impatient world of foreign exchange trading, *longer-term* could mean anywhere from as short as a week or a month to as long as a year, or possibly more. Most individuals trading foreign exchange on a retail basis do not have the patience to be position traders. This is somewhat unfortunate, as position trading can be one of the most profitable styles of trading due to the fact that many currencies tend to trend exceptionally well on a longer-term basis. Only those position traders who have the patience to stick with the trend and let their profits run are generally able to capitalize substantially on these longer-term price moves.

Unlike swing trading and day trading, which will both be discussed later in this chapter, position trading usually relies substantially on fundamental analysis, along with longer-term technical analysis. Other than in the realm of ultra-short-term news trading, which will also be discussed later in this chapter, fundamental analysis is usually geared toward longer-term price forecasts rather than toward the short-term swing-to-swing movements that are primarily the domain of technical analysis. As discussed in Chapter 4, fundamental analysis concerns itself with the economic conditions that drive the major market movements. These economic conditions, which include interest rates, inflation, and economic growth, help to determine the value of a national currency over time. The general direction of change in this currency value over the long run is what interests position traders the most.

As mentioned in the beginning of this chapter, position trading can be considered very similar to trend trading. One of the differences between these two approaches is the type of analysis that is generally emphasized. Whereas position traders may often rely to a significant extent on long-term fundamentals along with technicals, trend traders (or trend followers) are very often almost exclusively technical in nature. Of course, this generalization is far from a clear-cut delineation, but it describes the broad characteristics of these two approaches sufficiently. Similarly, carry trading, where traders hold interest-positive positions in order to benefit from both regular interest payments and exchange rate profits, can be considered yet another form of position trading. Both trend trading and carry trading will be discussed later in this chapter.

How exactly does a position trader in the foreign exchange market decide which position(s) to take? Although there are countless factors and nuances that may enter into the decision-making picture, the basic concept can be relatively simple. Forex position traders weigh strength and weakness in currencies by looking into a myriad of underlying fundamental and technical factors. They then establish positions in currency pairs according to these views. Here, the discussion will focus on the fundamental aspects of position trading. In the section on trend trading, the technical aspects will be discussed.

Let us suppose that a position trader performs ongoing analysis on economic conditions surrounding the major currencies, and decides that the U.S. dollar is indicating significant fundamental weakness going forward, while the euro is indicating significant fundamental strength going forward. This conclusion could have stemmed from any number and combination of information sources from both countries/regions, including comments on central bank policy by a bank president, the state of inflationary pressure in the economy, the recent rate of economic growth, the likelihood of an impending recession, and so on.

After this fundamental analysis is duly performed, the trader may decide that there is sufficient evidence supporting overall weakness in the U.S. dollar combined with overall strength in the euro, and that this will be the likeliest projected scenario for at least the next six months. The next step is for the position trader to seek to establish a long position in the EUR/USD currency pair, which simultaneously provides the trader with a long euro position and a short dollar position. This combined trade positioning fulfills the trader's fundamental outlook on both currencies.

Pinpointing the most advantageous trade entry timing, as well as setting risk-managed exit strategies, would then be best accomplished with the use of technical analysis. But the longer-term directional basis for the position trade is sufficiently served by fundamental analysis alone.

The true strength of position trading using fundamental analysis in this manner lies in the concept of pairing strength with weakness. This concept fits the foreign exchange market extremely well because of the simple fact that all currencies are traded in pairs, unlike in other financial trading markets. Since trading forex requires a directional commitment on two currencies for each trade, position trading with the strength/weakness model is perhaps the most logical fundamental method for approaching long-term foreign exchange trading. Buying one currency because it looks like it will become stronger is a good way to trade. But buying one currency because it looks like it will become stronger while simultaneously selling (or shorting) another currency because it looks like it will become weaker is an even better way to trade.

The first step in the process of forex position trading is to perform ongoing fundamental research and analysis on all of the major tradable currencies. This can be accomplished through careful scrutiny of central bank policy statements, objective assessments of economic growth factors, and close monitoring of global economic news. When the currencies with the strongest positive future prospects and the ones with the strongest negative future prospects at any given point in time are identified, the opposite currencies can then be paired.

So, for example, within a pool of well-researched currencies, let us suppose that AUD and JPY happen to be deemed the strongest potential gainers in the group for the foreseeable future, while the CAD and CHF are deemed to be the strongest potential losers. The opposites could then be paired together for potential position trades consisting of long AUD/CAD, short CAD/JPY, long AUD/CHF and/or short CHF/JPY. After these trades are entered with the help of technical analysis, the positions would then be held for as long as they continued to move in the correct general direction, disregarding minor corrective swings and market noise.

From the standpoint of disciplined trading, as will be discussed in Chapter 6, position trading may perhaps be the most difficult method for approaching the foreign exchange markets, especially for beginners. It requires a great deal of patience and faith in one's own analysis to weather the inevitable swings against one's entrenched positions, not to mention excellent risk and money management. But if mastered properly along with some well-planned entry and exit techniques, this style of trading can be one of the most effective methods for extracting long-term profits from the foreign exchange markets.

Swing Trading—Riding the Waves

Also among the most popular methods of trading forex, swing trading differs considerably from position trading in almost every way. For the most part, swing traders generally ignore fundamental information and concentrate almost exclusively on the technicals. The only time swing traders will generally pay any attention to the fundamentals is when they check the schedule for fundamental news announcements so that they can avoid trading during market-moving economic data releases.

Much like its label suggests, swing trading is all about trading swings, or turns, in the market. Any price action that occurs over time in any financial trading market will be made up of countless short- to medium-term swings both up and down. This will occur whether the market is in trending mode (overall price movement in one general direction) or ranging mode (sideways price action). Swing traders attempt to capitalize on all of these swings.

Another way in which swing trading differs considerably from position trading lies in the general duration of trades. Whereas position traders will attempt to ride a trend as long as it remains intact, swing traders will have slipped in and out of a long-term trend many times over before the trend is finally exhausted.

However, many traders like to define swing trading strictly in terms of the duration of each trade. Some would say that the ideal swing trade should be held for two to five days, while others may say it should be one to four days. This viewpoint is very common, but perhaps somewhat misinformed. Much more important than the duration of the trade are the goals and principles behind this method of foreign exchange trading. The primary goal of swing trading is to exploit the natural advances and declines that are inevitable in any market, regardless of the timeframe. The time span of the trade is infinitely less of a factor in defining successful swing trading than the timing of the trade. Timing is one of the primary keys to executing good swing trades. After executing a well-timed entry, the trader should then determine the duration of the trade by how much the market is willing to offer on that particular swing, and not by some arbitrarily predetermined period of time.

As a classic technical approach to the markets, swing trading utilizes the most salient aspects of technical analysis as its main tools. This includes the pillars of support and resistance, trend, momentum, and volatility. With these tools, swing traders tackle the markets by identifying short-term, tradable turns (or swings) within the context of a larger trend or trading range. In a trend, this could mean trading pullbacks in the direction of the trend. In a trading range, this could mean trading the up-and-down price oscillations between support and resistance. Specific technical tools used in swing trading include trendlines, horizontal support and resistance lines, moving averages, and oscillators. As for charting timeframes, perhaps the most popular ones for swing traders are generally anywhere from the one-hour chart (where each bar/candlestick is worth an hour of price movement) to the four-hour and daily charts.

Swing trading allows traders to pinpoint precise, high-probability entries and exits for each and every trade, based soundly upon the technicals. A typical swing trade begins with a perception by the trader that a market turn might be in the midst of occurring. This perception could be fueled by a host of different triggers, whether it is an oscillator reaching severely overbought or oversold, a price-oscillator divergence occurring (described later in this chapter), a reversal chart pattern forming (also described later in this chapter), a break of a trendline occurring, or price reaching a significant support/resistance level. Any or a combination of these events, or other technical indications, could trigger the trader's perception that an impending turn could potentially occur.

Once the initial perception is triggered, the prudent swing trader immediately searches for confirmation. For example, if the initial perception is triggered by a divergence indication, the trader will check to see if any other patterns, support/resistance levels and/or oscillators are confirming an impending swing. If there is indeed confirmation, the experienced swing trader would then consider possible entries and exits (stop losses and profit targets) to determine if the trade is viable from a risk/reward perspective (as discussed in Chapter 6).

Given the prevailing trade conditions, if the reward-to-risk ratio appears to be sound, the swing trader would then decide upon the size and leverage of the trade if these factors have not already been predetermined. The final step in the swing trading decision process would then be to prepare to enter the trade with either a market order or a stop/limit entry order. Simultaneously, the trader would also set stop loss and/or trailing stop parameters, as well as an appropriate profit target according to the trading plan.

For short- to medium-term timeframes, swing trading can potentially be a very-high-probability approach to forex. Price swings are extremely prevalent in every financial trading market and on every charting timeframe. The up and down swings occur naturally during all market conditions, whether in a trending market or a trading range. Moreover, setting risk management controls in the form of stop losses, as well as determining optimal risk/reward parameters, can be extremely precise and straightforward for the typical swing trade.

Day Trading—In and Out, Day In and Day Out

The majority of beginning forex traders try their hand first at day trading. This is perhaps due to the fact that this style of trading is generally the most exciting and fast-paced of the different styles. There are certainly traders who have made a consistently profitable living through day trading currencies, but it is definitely not as easy as it may initially appear to be.

Day trading is usually defined as the entering and exiting of positions within a single trading day. This means that few, if any, trades are held over to the next trading day. It also means that day traders must necessarily attempt to extract small profits from quick movements on the shortest of charting timeframes, usually anywhere from the 1-minute chart (where each bar/candlestick is worth one minute of price movement) to the 5-minute, 10-minute, 15-minute,

30-minute, and everything in between. Occasionally, timeframes as long as the 1-hour chart are used for day trading.

Trading on the shortest timeframes in this manner works well only if the trader possesses the requisite discipline, technique, and money management skills to overcome the formidable odds surrounding this style of trading. One rather considerable difficulty with short-term day trading is the fact that a necessarily small number of pips is targeted for each trade's profit objective, making the cost of the bid/ask spread a very significant prohibiting factor. For example, if a typical profit objective is around 20 pips for a day trade, a 3-pip spread alone accounts for an immediate handicap of 15% of the projected profit. This occurs even before there is actually any price movement on the trade. The day trader therefore has a distinct statistical disadvantage from the outset. In contrast, the 3-pip spread on a targeted 60-pip swing trade or a 300-pip position trade would represent an immediate handicap of only 5% or 1% of projected profit, respectively.

That being said, day trading can still be a viable method of approaching forex for experienced and determined traders. The techniques employed by day traders vary widely. Often, these techniques involve breakouts of short-term support and resistance levels. This could mean a breakout of a low volatility trading range, or a sharp move at the opening of an active currency market like London or New York. Breakouts are discussed in more depth later in the chapter.

Other times, day traders will trade purely based upon indicator confirmations. For example, a day trader may have a rule to open a long trade if the 5-period exponential moving average (EMA) crosses above the 20-period EMA, but only if the 14-period

Relative Strength Index (RSI) has also crossed above 30 and the slope of the MACD histogram is up. (Note: These trading rules were meant to serve as an arbitrary example, and were not actually tested as part of a trading strategy.)

Because day trading currencies can be extremely fast and intense, there is usually insufficient time or opportunity to perform discretionary market analysis in a leisurely manner. Therefore, more than with any other trading style, day trading often requires concrete trading rules that can be followed without much thinking on the part of the trader. Clear and simple rules that are meant to be followed to the letter generally work best for ultra short-term day traders. For these traders, quick thinking and quick reactions are among the most important traits to possess.

As mentioned, day trading currencies is often indicator-based. Traders may overlay several indicators on their price charts such as moving averages, Bollinger Bands, or a host of others. In addition, they will also frequently add an oscillator or two running vertically above or below price such as the MACD, RSI, or Stochastics. Using this type of methodology, trading foreign exchange becomes as rote and straightforward as waiting for the various indicators to point in the same direction at the same time. Although the rules here may be simple, however, this style of trading is anything but easy. It requires a great deal of discipline to follow strict, indicator-based day trading rules without allowing emotions to interfere in the process.

Besides indicator-based trading, many day traders will trade purely based upon breakouts of support and resistance. To denote these support and resistance levels, these traders may manually draw horizontal lines on their charts depicting levels where price turned or consolidated in the recent past. This method of visual determination is perhaps one of the most accurate ways of representing potential support and resistance. As mentioned in Chapter 3, a tenet of technical analysis is that over time, price will visit and turn at certain levels repeatedly (otherwise known as support/resistance).

Other popular short-term day trading methods for determining support and resistance include pivot points, Fibonacci retracements, and trendlines. Day traders will use the levels derived from these studies to identify either breakouts of the lines or bounces off the lines. All of these techniques will be discussed in more detail further on in this chapter.

Day trading appeals to the common human interest in immediate gratification. Many traders who gravitate toward day trading are lured by the illusory promise of instant profits for little effort. This particular promise is an empty one. Nevertheless, if approached in the correct manner with good technique and excellent risk/money management, day trading can potentially become a profitable pursuit.

Trend Trading—Going with the Flow

Day trading, swing trading, and position trading, as just described, are general approaches to trading foreign exchange. This trend trading section begins a more in-depth look at the methods and strategies commonly used by foreign exchange traders.

Trend trading, or trend following, is very similar to the general position trading approach used by longer-term traders/investors. The main distinction, as mentioned earlier, lies in the types of analysis that are generally emphasized. Position traders will usually utilize both technical and fundamental analysis in their decision-making processes. In contrast, trend followers will commonly employ technical analysis almost exclusively.

The goal of trend trading is to jump on a trend when the direction is technically clear, and ride it as long as it is intact. Technical trend following purists may identify uptrends when clear higher lows and higher highs begin appearing on a chart. By the same token, downtrends are identified by lower highs and lower lows. Trendlines and parallel trend channels will often be used to outline these trends on a chart.

Another method of measuring the existence and strength of a trend is the use of moving averages, where the slope of a moving average may indicate whether there is a current uptrend, downtrend, or neither. Within a trend-trading context, moving averages can also be used to give crossover signals (as described in Chapter 3). Using this technique, if price crossed above a certain moving average it would be a buy signal, while a cross below would be a sell signal. Alternatively, a cross of a shorter moving average above a longer moving average would be a buy signal, while a cross below would be a sell signal. Moving averages are often used in this way, but the difficulty lies in the frequent false signals, where several unprofitable crosses occur in succession, otherwise known as whipsaw.

Yet another trend measurement tool that is widely used, but arguably weaker than the prior two methods, is the Average Directional Index (ADX), which oscillates to display the strength and existence of a trend on a currency chart. Many other indicators and studies are also used to identify trending conditions, but the three methods just mentioned are probably the most common. Additionally, breakouts in the direction of the general trend are another way of confirming trend continuation, but this will be discussed further in the section on breakout trading.

Once a trend is identified and measured using technical studies, the stage of the trend needs to be identified. Clearly, getting in at the beginning or middle of a trend run is vastly preferable to getting in late. Although there are no clear-cut delineations among the three stages, each stage can be discerned by its general characteristics.

If higher lows and higher highs begin occurring right after a well-defined downtrend or prolonged price consolidation, it could be a sign that an uptrend is in its early stage. Prudent trend traders may prefer to avoid entry at these first signs of trend change. In hindsight, this stage represents the best possible entry point, but at the time of decision it is full of uncertainty.

When the trend moves onto its middle stage, it is considered to be well-established with consistent prior evidence that price is making progress in one direction. It is at this point that many trend traders will jump on the trend, fueling it even further in the same direction. From a day trading or swing trading perspective, this type of entry in the middle of a trend is simply too late. From a position trading and trend trading perspective, however, it can be considered a sensible entry targeting long-term profits.

When it comes to the late stage of a trend, most of the major market players are already in position and looking to take profits. This late stage is perhaps the worst possible time to enter into a trend. But how would a trader know if this stage has been reached, or if the trend still has enough momentum to move much further? The answer to this question is difficult. There really is no way of knowing definitively until one can look back in hindsight and pinpoint the very end of the trend on a chart. At the same time, however, many clues will appear on the chart in real-time that hint at the near-end of a trend, including failures to reach higher highs in an uptrend (or lower lows in a downtrend), prolonged consolidations, and significantly diminished volatility. In any event, it is much better to play it safe by avoiding potential late stage entries altogether rather than risk buying at the highs or selling at the lows.

Once a trend and its stage have been identified, the next step for a trend trader is to decide on the timing and location of entry. For trend traders, this decision is not nearly as crucial as it is for shorter-term swing traders and day traders. Riding long-term trends is all about letting profits run as far as possible. With this mentality, trend traders are not as concerned about pinpointing a perfectly timed entry as a shorter-term trader might be. That being said, however, the better the entry the better the potential profit picture. Therefore, trend traders generally prefer to enter into a trend at high probability locations within the trend.

As shown in Exhibit 5.1, this would entail buying on the dips in an uptrend, or the temporary downward retracements within the overall uptrend. During a downtrend, it would entail short-selling on the rallies, or the temporary upward retracements within the overall downtrend. These areas constitute high probability entries for a very clear reason. In the case of an uptrend, buying "cheap" when price is steadily appreciating could perhaps be considered the most intelligent way to conduct trades in any type of business. The same general principle holds true, but in the opposite direction, for downtrends.

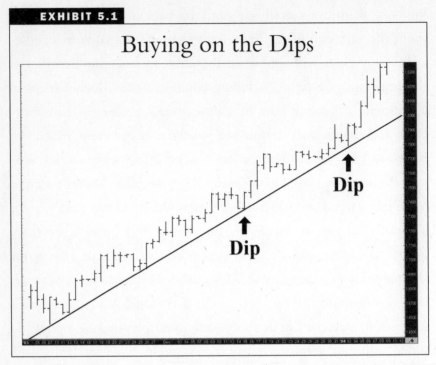

EXHIBIT 5.1

Buying on the Dips

Source: FX Solutions – FX AccuCharts

Once a trend has been entered, the trend trader must manage the position, albeit not as actively as a shorter-term trader might need to. It should be kept in mind here that the primary principle of trend trading is to let profits run while cutting losses short. This is the cornerstone of long-term trend following. With short-term swing trading and day trading, letting profits run is much less of a focus because these types of traders specialize in exploiting relatively minor price fluctuations. In contrast, trend traders are generally not so quick to take profits. These longer-term traders need to establish an excellent reward-to-risk ratio (as will be discussed in Chapter 6) in order for their few large profits to surpass the many small losses that are incurred during up-and-down whipsaws and false trend moves. So when a good, strong trend is found, the trend trader must ride it for all it is worth.

This means that perhaps the best way to manage established trend positions is through the use of trailing stop losses, whether manual or automated. These dynamic stop losses follow price such that profits are locked in as the position accumulates gains. With an automated trailing stop loss, the market is followed by a certain number of pips predetermined by the trader. A manual trailing stop loss is often a more preferred method of managing a trend trade. In an uptrend situation, for example, the trader would actually move the stop loss manually. A logical location for each move of the stop loss would be right below the last swing low (or dip). If price continues up, more gains are locked in, and the trailing stop loss gets moved to progressively higher dips. If price breaks below the last dip, however, it is a solid indication that the uptrend might possibly be ending. The manual trailing stop loss then promptly takes the trader out of the position, realizing all of the accumulated profits.

Other ways to manage trend trades besides using trailing stop losses include scaling in and scaling out of position. Scaling into position entails entering initially with a small, fractional trade size, and then adding onto the position as the trend develops further. This can be a great way to test the waters without being fully committed from the outset. If the trend fails initially, the loss is not excessive. If, however, the trend develops significantly, a full-sized position can be quickly scaled in.

Scaling out is just the opposite. Once a full position has matured, and there are indications of a possible waning of trend momentum, parts of the position may be closed in succession. The logic of this strategy is to lock in and realize profits on part of the position while allowing another part to take advantage of any further remaining momentum.

Finally, if the trend trade is not exited due to price hitting a stop loss (whether static or trailing) or to the trader scaling out of position, a trade exit may also be made when a profit target is hit. In initially setting the profit target, the trend trader should take into consideration a minimum reward-to-risk ratio for this type of trade, as well as the prevailing market conditions evident on the chart. On longer-term trend trades, the reward-to-risk ratio, as will be discussed in Chapter 6, should preferably be set as high as possible. Therefore, the profit target should ideally be set to several times the magnitude of the initial stop loss. This, by definition, is the manifestation of the popular trading proverb, "Let your profits run and cut your losses short." At the same time, however, the market will give only what it has to give. In other words, a high reward-to-risk ratio cannot be forced, as profit potential depends solely upon market conditions. For this reason, the trailing stop loss is generally the preferred method for exiting trend trades over the more arbitrary profit target method.

Trend trading is one of the most effective strategies for approaching foreign exchange trading. Many of the most successful and well-known traders, whether they trade stocks, futures, or currencies, consider themselves long-term trend traders. It is perhaps the best single method for capturing major currency price movements, especially since foreign exchange is generally considered to be a market that trends frequently.

Range Trading—Between a Rock and a Hard Place

If the foreign exchange market trends often, what is it doing when it is not trending? Most likely, it is trading in a range. Ranges are periods when price moves up and down without a clear directional trend. Some would characterize the price action during a range as "sideways," or horizontal. Generally speaking, this kind of directionless price movement is bounded on a top extreme by a resistance line and on a bottom extreme by a support line. Exhibit 5.2 illustrates a typical trading range.

It is between these support and resistance boundaries that the range trading opportunities lie. Range trading simply involves

EXHIBIT 5.2

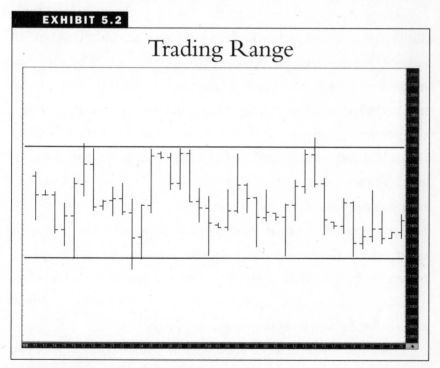

Trading Range

Source: FX Solutions — FX AccuCharts

identifying and capitalizing upon the turns within a horizontal trading range. These turns are also considered swings, so the techniques of range trading are often an important component of a swing trader's repertoire.

While range trading may be a popular strategy, some traders, especially those that concentrate on following trends, consider it to be a much lower probability method. This is primarily because of the fact that the upside in range trading is necessarily capped at the other side of the range. By definition, range traders do not let their profits run the way trend traders do. As this is true, range traders can increase their potential upside by setting a minimum threshold in terms of the height of the ranges that they are willing to trade.

For example, a 20-pip range that forms on the GBP/USD pair during Asian session is not really worth range trading. This type of range is best reserved for breakout trading, which will be discussed in the next section. The height of the range is just too diminutive to make it worthwhile as a range trading opportunity. In other words, the potential profit is not sufficient to justify the risk. A 300-pip range, however, can certainly offer range traders an abundance of good potential trading opportunities that can be very worthwhile. If stop losses are always placed just beyond the support or resistance level from which a range trade is initiated, a profit target (on the other side of the range) that is further away would clearly offer a higher probability trade from a risk/reward perspective. Therefore, a prudent range trading approach should include some minimum criteria for the height of the range.

Once the height of a potential range is established by at least two approximate touches of both support and resistance, preparation for range trading can begin. Most range traders will use the common horizontal lines on their charts to denote the support and resistance levels in a range. Some, however, will use dynamic bands, most notably the Bollinger Bands, to outline these levels. Tools like the Bollinger Bands can certainly be useful in trading ranges that do not possess very strictly defined upper and lower bounds. With the use of Bollinger Bands, however, a range trader should also monitor the slope of the simple moving average running through the middle of the Bands to ensure that it is indeed flat or near-flat. Only in this way can the trader be adequately confident that a horizontal range is indeed in place.

On the establishment of the range using one of the methods mentioned, the range trader might then simply use a common oscillator like Stochastics or RSI to help indicate potential turns at or near resistance and support. The most common method of reading these oscillators is to identify the point at which they cross the line exiting overbought or oversold, which denotes a possible impending turn. This is illustrated in Exhibit 5.3.

Besides the oscillator indications, another turn confirmation can be found at the break of an intra-range trendline, as shown in Exhibit 5.4.

Although requiring a trendline break confirmation in this fashion will almost always lead to a relatively late trade entry, it can present valuable evidence that a turn within the range has indeed occurred. A tighter stop loss can then be placed on the other side of the trendline break as opposed to the other side of the range support/resistance.

Range trading can be an effective method for trading foreign exchange during periods when there is no discernible trend in the market. During these periods when price tends to bounce

EXHIBIT 5.3

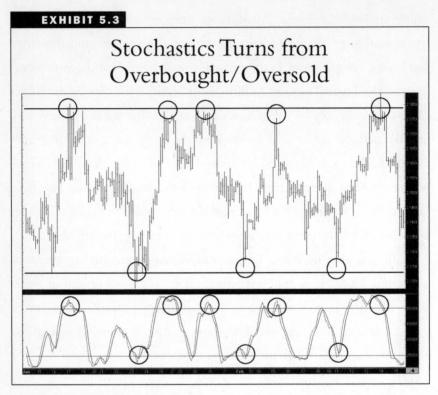

Stochastics Turns from Overbought/Oversold

Source: FX Solutions - FX AccuCharts

repeatedly between horizontal resistance and support, traders must either utilize methods similar to those described above, or stay out of the market altogether. If an established range has sufficient height, trading the bounces can be a potentially effective approach to sustained nontrending market conditions.

Breakout Trading (and Fading)—Shooting for the Stars

Where range trading attempts to capitalize on turns that respect established support and resistance levels, breakout trading is just

EXHIBIT 5.4

Intra-Range Trendline Breakouts

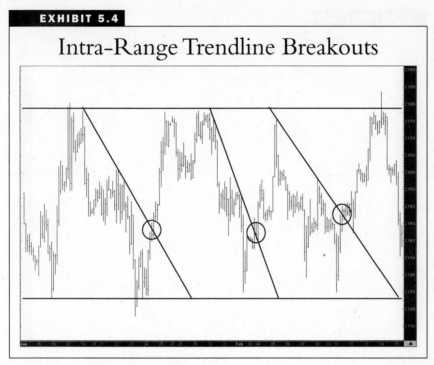

Source: FX Solutions – FX AccuCharts

the opposite. Foreign exchange traders who specialize in breakouts spend their time looking for violations of support and resistance. Exhibit 5.5 illustrates a typical forex breakout opportunity.

To many, breakout trading makes more sense than any other method of trading, as a breakout with strong momentum can potentially yield a great deal of pips for the relatively small amount of risk involved. For this reason, a lot of traders gravitate immediately to trading breakouts. But these traders soon realize that it is not as easy as it may initially appear to be. This is because many of the major breakouts that occur in today's foreign exchange markets tend to be false breakouts. This is when a breakout occurs without any follow

EXHIBIT 5.5

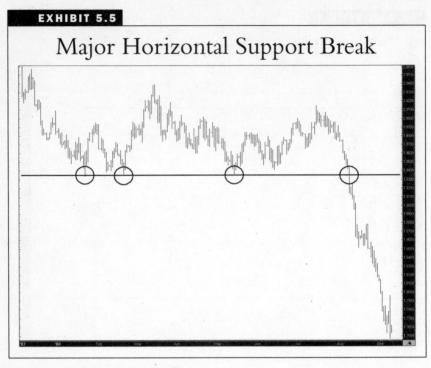

Major Horizontal Support Break

Source: FX Solutions – FX AccuCharts

through and then reverses, trapping all of the breakout traders who hastily jumped on the opportunity.

False breakouts of this nature tend to be of two types. The first can be called a "fakeout," where a support/resistance line is breached slightly, but then price just turns back and goes in the opposite direction as soon as most of the breakout traders get trapped. This type of false break is akin to price respecting support/resistance after breaching it only slightly. The second type of false break is called a premature breakout, where a slight breakout occurs, then turns around to go back in the opposite direction, and then finally turns once again to perform a true breakout on a subsequent

152

attempt. Both of these types of false breaks can be extremely frustrating for breakout traders.

As a reaction to the proliferation of false breaks on currency charts, some former breakout traders have transformed into what are called breakout "faders," where they fade, or trade against, major breakouts. Trading against a dominant movement in this way can also be a risky strategy, but with the proper risk controls and money management in place, it can be an effective approach in many instances.

Whether a trader fades or trades a breakout, the techniques used to denote relevant support and resistance levels is identical. The simplest, and perhaps most reliable, method involves manually drawing horizontal lines on a chart that correspond to previous market turns. As explained in Chapter 3, horizontal support and resistance are partly derived from traders' collective memory of a given price level, and whether the general consensus considers that level relatively high or relatively low. If a price level is considered relatively low (support), buying activity at that level should occur. Conversely, if a price level is considered relatively high (resistance), selling activity should occur. When these activities occur on a major basis by many market participants, the end result should generally be a turn at support or resistance.

Therefore, drawing a horizontal line extending from a previous turn makes a lot of sense. Traders' memories of relative price levels are clearest at the levels of previous market turns. That is one of the reasons that we frequently see price turn repeatedly at a certain level over a prolonged period of time. Exhibit 5.6 illustrates the technique of manually drawing horizontal support and resistance lines at market turns.

In the case of breakouts, the logic is equally simple. The reasoning is that price should respect previously established support and

EXHIBIT 5.6

Manually Drawn Horizontal Lines

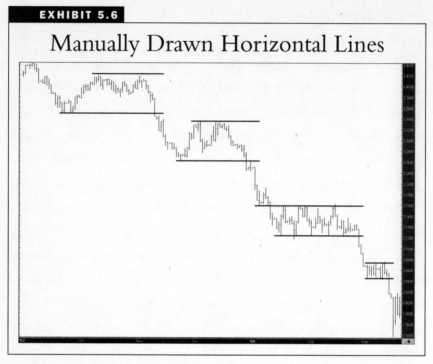

Source: FX Solutions – FX AccuCharts

resistance levels under normal circumstances, but if there is a strong enough catalyst for pushing price to break a given level, that breach should carry enough momentum to take price to the next further support/resistance level. If the breakout level in question is a very-long-term or all-time high or low, where a further established support/resistance level does not exist, the assumption is that price will subsequently make new highs/lows somewhere significantly beyond the broken level. As we saw in the case of false breakouts, however, this assumption does not always hold true.

Besides the technique of manually drawn horizontal lines for denoting support and resistance levels, there are also several other

EXHIBIT 5.7

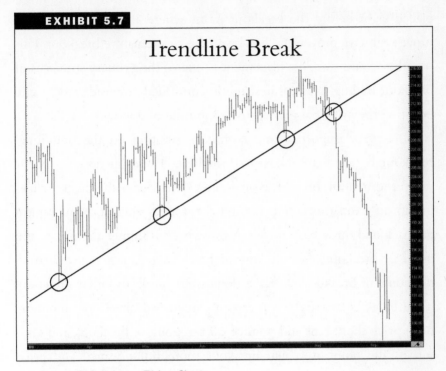

Trendline Break

Source: FX Solutions – FX AccuCharts

methods available that can be used in breakout trading. These other methods, however, will usually yield different price levels than the horizontal line technique. They include: dynamic trendlines (as illustrated in Exhibit 5.7), chart patterns (described later in this chapter), pivot points and Fibonacci retracements (also described later in this chapter), and moving averages.

However support and resistance are measured, the concept of trading breakouts is straightforward. A trader customarily enters the breakout trade beyond the actual breakout point, balancing the goal of avoiding a false breakout with the goal of getting in as early as possible for a larger profit potential. A hard stop loss is generally placed right before the breakout point where, if it is hit, the price move will have proven itself to be a false or premature breakout. This straightforward stop loss placement is one of the primary strengths of breakout trading, as it ensures tightly controlled downside risk, while boosting the potential reward-to-risk profile of the trade.

One very important and common variation on the traditional breakout is called the pullback/throwback. These phenomena occur when momentum on a breakout wanes shortly after the break, resulting in an extra move. See Exhibit 5.8 for an illustration of typical pullback and throwback moves. A throwback is simply a return to the point of breakout after an upward break. A pullback is a return to the point of breakdown after a downward break. In either direction, if the break is true (which means it carries real directional momentum) price should hit and bounce off the point of breakout, and then surpass the point at which breakout momentum waned and price turned. On a true break, price should then continue in the breakout

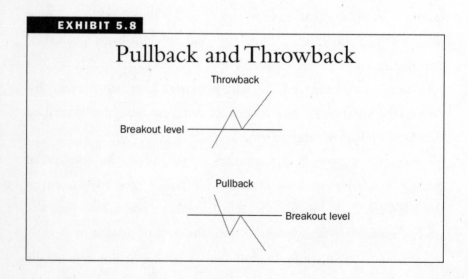

EXHIBIT 5.8

Pullback and Throwback

direction as if the pullback or throwback never occurred. Some prudent breakout traders will wait for a pullback/throwback before getting in on a breakout trade. Traders who do so may miss some potential trading opportunities (as many breakouts do not have pullbacks or throwbacks), but that extra patience often pays off in better-positioned breakout trades with somewhat reduced risk.

Like range trading, breakout trading is a very popular strategy for approaching forex. Breakouts occur frequently on currency charts. Whether these breakouts are real or false, however, is the difficulty in implementing this methodology. But since the nature of breakout trading inherently possesses an extremely straightforward and beneficial method for setting optimal risk management controls (stop losses), trading in this manner can be a very high probability method for approaching the foreign exchange markets.

EXECUTIVE INSIGHT

Ed Ponsi

Ed Ponsi, president of FXEducator.com and author of *Forex Patterns and Probabilities,* is well-known in the industry as a top trader, money manager, and forex trading educator. He has advised hedge funds, institutional traders, and individual traders of all levels of skill and experience, and has become one of the most sought-after lecturers in the financial world.

Ponsi states:

"Regarding technique, I'm primarily a trend trader. I look for situations where the technicals mesh with the fundamentals—if there is a clear trend in place, and if the fundamentals confirm what I see on the chart, I'm going to try to grab a chunk of that trend.

One thing I'm very cautious about is trading the breakout—if the trend is moving upwards, I want to go long but I don't want to buy a currency as it's hitting new highs. Because there are so many false breakouts in forex trading, my strategy is to try to catch the pullbacks. That way, even if the currency pair fails to break through, there is still some potential for profit when the pair reaches resistance.

One of my favorite situations is a false breakout that moves against the trend. These types of breakouts have a high failure rate, and they also set the stage for a 'slingshot' trade in the opposite direction. It's a great setup, and I'm constantly looking for it.

If the trend is strong enough, I might not use a target at all; instead, I'll trail a stop. I like to trail stops manually, moving them strategically instead of automatically. That way, I can keep my stop beneath a trend line or moving average, instead of moving it to an arbitrary location—which is often exactly what happens when we use automatic trailing stops."

Pattern Trading—Playing with Shapes

As mentioned in the previous section, pattern trading may be considered one form of breakout trading, depending upon which type of chart pattern one might be referring to. There are essentially two general types of chart patterns. First are the several multibar shapes that together constitute one of the pillars of Western-style technical analysis. These formations generally represent price consolidation, and include triangles, flags, pennants, wedges, rectangles, and head-and-shoulders, among others. Many of the most important of these patterns are illustrated and described in detail in Chapter 3. For the most part, all of these patterns are generally traded when a breakout of one type or another occurs. Conversely, the second type of chart pattern—candlestick patterns (also described in Chapter 3)—are not tied as closely with breakout trading.

When speaking of pattern breakouts, it is helpful to delineate which patterns are more often considered continuation patterns and which ones are more often considered reversal patterns. These delineations are far from rules, as any pattern could act as a continuation pattern or a reversal pattern, or neither (e.g., prolonged consolidation after breakout). Traditionally, though, most patterns have fulfilled certain roles that historically have been somewhat reliable to a certain extent. A continuation pattern is simply a consolidation formation where price exits, or breaks out of, the pattern in the direction of the trend that prevailed prior to the formation. Conversely, a reversal pattern is a consolidation formation where price exits, or breaks out of, the pattern in the opposite direction of the trend that prevailed prior to the formation.

As indicated in Chapter 3, of the most common patterns found on currency charts, those that are generally considered reversal formations include double tops/bottoms, triple tops/bottoms, and head-and-shoulders tops/bottoms. Those that are most often considered continuation patterns include flags, pennants, triangles, wedges, and rectangles, among others.

When a continuation pattern approaches breakout on the side of the pattern that would denote a continuation, technical traders wait patiently for a break. At this point, it is treated as a breakout trade with a similar type of entry and stop-loss placement as with standard support/resistance breakout trades. The same holds true for reversal patterns when price approaches breakout on the side of the pattern that would denote a reversal. But in actuality, any type of breakout of these patterns, whether in the direction of continuation or reversal, is an eagerly watched and traded event.

One added benefit of trading pattern breakouts lies in the precise structuring of profit targets. Most patterns have a built-in profit target after breakout. A good example is the well-known head-and-shoulders pattern. As shown in Exhibit 5.9, after price breaks the neckline, the traditional signal for a trade, the target is derived by measuring the height of the pattern from the top of the head to the neckline, and then projecting that height from the neckline break down for the profit target. Similarly, for a rectangle consolidation pattern, the height of the rectangle is projected up or down to derive a profit target after breakout. Triangles, flags, pennants, and other chart patterns also have convenient, built-in targets.

EXHIBIT 5.9

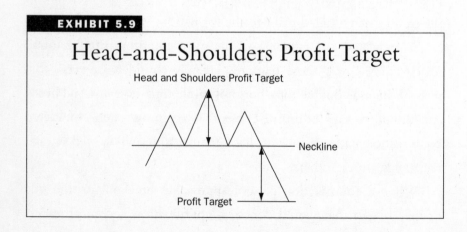

Head-and-Shoulders Profit Target

Head and Shoulders Profit Target

Neckline

Profit Target

In contrast with Western-style chart patterns, Japanese-style candlestick patterns (the most important of which are described in Chapter 3) are generally smaller chart formations that are not usually considered self-sufficient trading signals. Rather, candlestick patterns are more often utilized as important trade confirmation tools that are used in conjunction with other analytical methods. For example, a hammer candle that occurs after a steep, well-defined downtrend should not be taken by itself as a reversal signal to buy at the low. But if this candle occurs right at a well-established support level, the hammer can certainly represent a strong confirmation that a potential long trade may be in order.

Pattern trading is very similar to general support/resistance breakout trading in terms of entries and exits, but with the added benefit of clear-cut profit targets. Patterns appear very frequently on foreign currency charts, and can be found on all charting timeframes. Through diligent chart-watching practice, any foreign exchange trader can learn to spot even the most comprehensive pattern trading opportunities at a glance.

Fibonacci and Pivot Point Trading—Magic Numbers and Self-Fulfilling Prophecies

Also sharing some similar characteristics with general support/resistance trading, the use of Fibonacci levels and pivot points are often considered by their adherents as complete, self-contained trading strategies. The origins of these two methodologies are far from intertwined with each other, but they are grouped together here because they are commonly traded and analyzed in a similar fashion.

The horizontal price levels that are generated through Fibonacci and pivot points are calculated using different methods, but they both produce mathematically derived support and resistance levels that traders may use either as indicators of possible retracement turns or as zones to watch for breakouts.

A substantial component of what makes these tools work surprisingly well under diverse market conditions is the simple fact that many traders, both large and small, utilize both Fibonacci and pivot points in their trading. Therefore, the levels derived from these popular tools become a sort of self-fulfilling prophecy. This is where significant price action often occurs around these levels due to the simple fact that many traders are watching and reacting to these price levels. This phenomenon contributes to their frequent effectiveness and accuracy in describing market movement.

As discussed in Chapter 3 on technical analysis tools, the mathematical theory now generally known as Fibonacci Theory is widely considered to have originated from a 13th century Italian mathematician appropriately named, Leonardo Fibonacci. He calculated a sequence of numbers that led to the discovery of the Golden Ratio, 1.618, which is a proportion that advocates say can be found in nature, science, music, and even financial markets. Derived from this ratio and its inverse of 0.618 are the Fibonacci percentages commonly used in technical analysis today. There are several modern charting tools based on these percentages that have been created expressly for analyzing price charts, of which the most popular is the standard Fibonacci retracement tool.

The most common Fibonacci retracement percentages, as shown in Exhibit 5.10, include 23.6%, 38.2%, 50%, and 61.8%. Of these, the latter three are perhaps the most closely followed by traders and

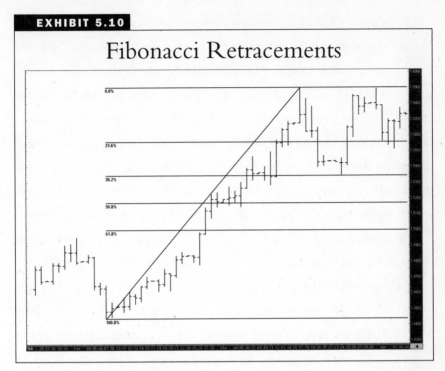

EXHIBIT 5.10

Fibonacci Retracements

Source: FX Solutions – FX AccuCharts

analysts. Very often, one will read commentary from an analyst in the financial news proclaiming that price is approaching the 38.2% retracement level, and that something important, like a turn, could occur at this key level. Such is the widespread popularity of Fibonacci retracements.

As mentioned earlier, Fibonacci retracements are customarily traded in one of two ways—either as a breakout opportunity or as a retracement turn (a bounce). Both are viable methods of trading forex that have built-in and clear-cut locations for stop-loss placement, much like all support/resistance trading techniques. In addition, Fibonacci levels can also be used as profit targets for existing open trades.

Similar to Fibonacci retracements in both look and functionality are pivot points. As described in Chapter 3, pivot points originated long ago in other financial markets. They are derived mathematically from the previous day's key data points, including the high, low, and close. The main pivot point price level, labeled "PP," is calculated by taking the mean (average) of the high, low, and close from the prior day's price action. From the PP, four other primary pivot points are calculated, two above and two below the main PP. The levels above are R1 and R2, where "R" stands for resistance. The levels below are S1 and S2, where "S" stands for support. Often, this pivot point structure is extended even further to R3 and S3.

Following are the calculations for the most common daily pivot points. Although a pivot point calculator may readily be found online, and is also a standard component of many charting software packages, it is still useful to know how these important levels are derived. Beginning with the middle Pivot Point that is calculated from the previous day's key price points, as per the following calculations, the resulting support and resistance levels are subsequently derived.

R3 (Resistance 3) = Yesterday's High + 2(PP − Yesterday's Low)

R2 (Resistance 2) = PP + (RI − SI)

R1 (Resistance 1) = 2 × PP − Yesterday's Low

PP (Pivot Point) = (Yesterday's High + Yesterday's Low + Yesterday's Close) ÷ 3

S1 (Support 1) = 2 × PP - Yesterday's High

S2 (Support 2) = PP − (R1 − S1)

S3 (Support 3) = Yesterday's Low − 2(Yesterday's High − PP)

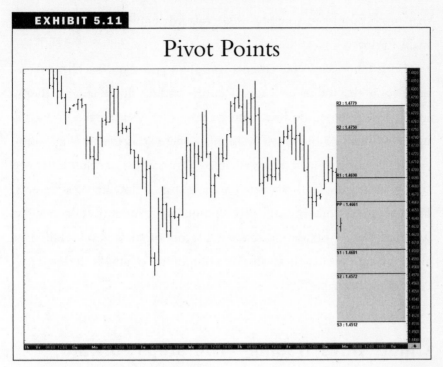

EXHIBIT 5.11

Pivot Points

R3 : 1.4779

R2 : 1.4750

R1 : 1.4690

PP : 1.4661

S1 : 1.4601

S2 : 1.4572

S3 : 1.4512

Source: FX Solutions – FX AccuCharts

Traders can calculate the current day's relevant pivot points using these calculations, based upon the previous day's price data, and then plot the levels using horizontal lines on a currency price chart. Exhibit 5.11 illustrates the calculated levels plotted on a chart. Once these levels are calculated and plotted, they are used in much the same way as Fibonacci retracements. Breakouts or bounces may be traded, and they are often also used as profit targets. Traders also use pivot points as reference levels to provide guidance as to whether the current price is relatively low or relatively high within its expected range for the day. If price is near the day's S2, for example, traders may look for long trading opportunities with the view that price should reasonably move towards equilibrium around the main PP level.

Both Fibonacci retracements and pivot points are excellent technical tools that often encompass entire trading disciplines in themselves. Mostly based on breakouts or bounces (whether the bounce is up off support or down off resistance), these strategic trading methodologies can also lend very valuable confirmation to other currency trading strategies. Both known for their large following of adherents, Fibonacci retracements and pivot points are frequently effective for just that reason—traders actually trade off of these levels. This fact alone makes these tools a valuable component of any trader's technical trading arsenal.

Elliott Wave Trading—Two Steps Forward, One Step Back

Related to Fibonacci Theory, Elliott Wave Theory also claims an enormous following of practitioners. As briefly discussed in Chapter 3, Elliott Wave is named after Ralph Nelson Elliott, who asserted that price movement is predictable and can be classified into a series of identifiable waves. The basic structure is five waves comprising the trend movement and three waves comprising the corrective (or countertrend) movement. Furthermore, within each of these waves is a smaller sub-wave structure that also adheres to the 5/3 pattern, depending upon whether the wave is with the larger trend or against it. So the basic 5/3 wave pattern remains intact on every magnitude, from the longest-term to the shortest-term, and each wave

EXHIBIT 5.12

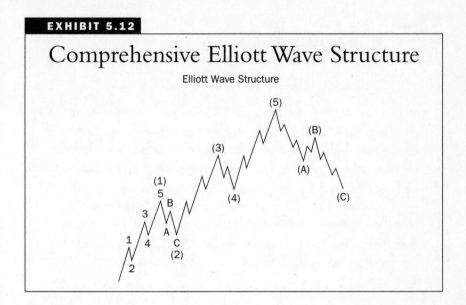

Comprehensive Elliott Wave Structure

Elliott Wave Structure

pattern exists within the context of a larger wave pattern while also encompassing many smaller wave patterns. Perhaps the best way to understand this principle is through a visual representation. Exhibit 5.12 provides an illustration of a comprehensive Elliott Wave structure.

There are three primary guidelines of a trend pattern in Elliott Wave, according to its founder. Within the context of the 5-wave trend cycle, as shown in Exhibit 5.12, Wave 2 never moves beyond the beginning of Wave 1, Wave 3 is never the shortest of the five waves, and Wave 4 never enters the price span of Wave 1. Beyond these strictly observed principles, there are numerous nuances surrounding Elliott Wave theory that are well beyond the scope of this book. An explanation of how practitioners view the real-world implications of each wave, though, should help illustrate how Elliott Wave traders approach the foreign exchange markets.

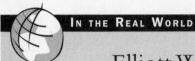

IN THE REAL WORLD

Elliott Wave Trading

In practice, trading according to Elliott Wave principles is primarily about identifying market turns, whether those turns are merely minor retracements within a dominant trend or if they are major market reversals. Within a typical 5-wave dominant trend pattern, each wave represents a certain market psychology. The same is true of each wave within the 3-wave corrective pattern. Following is a description of each wave's significance within the more readily identifiable 5-wave trend. This particular description will depict a dominant UPtrend. The same principles apply, but in reverse, for dominant DOWNtrends.

Wave 1: Within the context of a brand new uptrend, the currency pair in question is still considered by the majority of market participants and analysts to be entrenched in the previously prevailing downtrend. Therefore, at the time that the trend reversal occurs, it can often be extremely difficult to identify the fact that a new trend is indeed beginning. At this point, buying activity is only a trickle, as contrarian traders begin accumulating inexpensively at or near the lows. This initial move within the new uptrend later turns out to be a significant push that becomes progressively more obvious as the first wave ends.

Wave 2: After the initial push in the new direction, this second wave constitutes, among other actions, profit-taking by those who participated in the first wave. This correction should not, however, reach past the beginning of the first wave. Not only does this second wave represent profit-taking, but this corrective move is also partly caused by the many traders who are acting on their belief that the market is still embedded within the previous downtrend.

Wave 3: This wave usually constitutes the strongest and largest move within the 5-wave pattern. At the very least, it should never be the shortest. Throughout this wave, traders, analysts, and the media become progressively more bullish and committed to the new trend in the currency pair. By the end of this third wave, a buying frenzy among the masses may have developed, generally pushing the pair to new heights in a swift and steep manner. This wave should extend well past the end of the first wave.

Wave 4: Representing a corrective pullback move before the final push, this wave is generally not as strong as the other waves, and often tends to move in a sideways, consolidative fashion. Many Elliott Wave practitioners consider the end of this wave as an ideal place to enter a position on a pullback (or "dip"). This trade setup would be a long trade, in the direction of both the final wave and the dominant trend. One primary rule is that this wave should never enter the price region of the first wave.

Wave 5: This is the final push in the direction of the main trend. At this point, bullish sentiment on the currency pair is approaching a peak. Analysts, traders, and the media are generally extremely positive, fueling even more buying activity. During the middle of this wave, novice traders get carried away with all of this bullishness and begin joining the buying crowd at this late stage, if they have not done so already. During this last wave, only contrarians quietly begin to take profits on their long positions and start to short-sell. This process gains momentum to culminate in a peak high, and ultimately the beginnings of a corrective 3-wave pattern.

Elliott Wave trading is one of the more difficult strategies to master, as it requires a great deal of practice and experience in order to be able to identify waves effectively under different market conditions. As many professional Elliott Wave traders will agree, however, learning to trade these waves can potentially be very rewarding.

Divergence Trading—Separate Paths

Also an effective analytical tool if used in the correct manner, price-oscillator divergences have long been acknowledged by technical traders and analysts as a solid indicator of potential impending price reversals. Of course, by no means should it be inferred in any way that divergences will always predict a reversal, or even that they are correct a majority of the time. But well-defined price-oscillator divergences, especially on longer-term charts, can be surprisingly accurate in many instances. Furthermore, catching a major price reversal at the correct time can be so potentially profitable that only a few accurate divergences are needed to offset the inevitable false signals.

Price-oscillator divergence can be spotted with just two elements on a price chart. The first element is price, while the second element is an oscillator that runs either above or below price. This second element could be Stochastics, RSI, MACD or any similar oscillator as described in Chapter 3. A divergence occurs when there is an imbalance between the price element and the oscillator element. They begin to go separate ways and start telling opposite stories. This is when the oscillator is providing a strong hint that price may be losing its current momentum, and a change in price direction may therefore be impending.

So, for example, bearish divergence (which hints at an impending reversal back down) occurs when price hits a higher high while the oscillator hits a corresponding lower high. Exhibit 5.13 displays a typical instance of bearish divergence.

The indication after a clear bearish divergence signal is that price may soon turn and go back down as the higher high in price loses its upward momentum and begins falling.

EXHIBIT 5.13

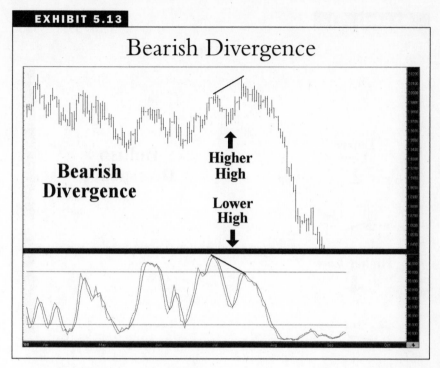

Source: FX Solutions – FX AccuCharts

Bullish divergence (which hints at an impending reversal back up) occurs when price hits a lower low while the oscillator hits a corresponding higher low. Exhibit 5.14 displays a typical instance of bullish divergence.

The indication after a clear bullish divergence signal is that price may soon turn and go back up as the lower low in price loses its downward momentum and begins rising.

Divergences are often used as hints, or early indications, of possible turns and reversals. Much less often are they employed exclusively as a full-fledged, self-sufficient trading strategy. But used in

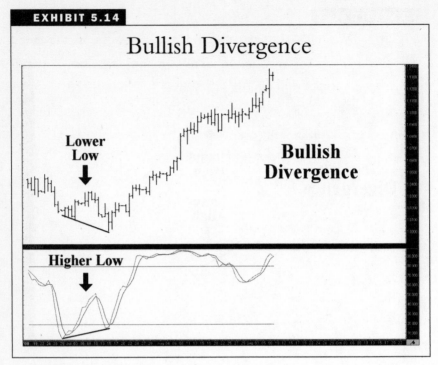

EXHIBIT 5.14

Source: FX Solutions – FX AccuCharts

conjunction with other trading tools, divergences can often be a remarkably effective method for helping to time major market turns.

Multiple Timeframe Trading—Timing Is Everything

A trading method used very extensively by many foreign exchange traders involves the use of multiple timeframes. To trade in this manner, a trader might first look at a long-term timeframe like a monthly or weekly chart to determine the overall direction of the trend, if any. If a decisive long-term trend is in place, the trader should only trade in this direction.

Then, the trader may drill down to a shorter timeframe like the daily or 4-hour chart to look for dips, or pullbacks, in the trend. As mentioned in the section on trend trading, these are counter-trend moves that provide an advantageous location to enter in the direction of the trend. For example, in a strong long-term uptrend, a minor downward retracement would represent a potential high probability entry to get in on the trend at a good price.

Finally, the trader may drill down even further to an even shorter timeframe like the 30-minute or 15-minute chart to pinpoint and time exact entries. For example, if a retracement in an uptrend is identified on the 4-hour chart, the trader could go down to the 15-minute chart to wait for a resistance breakout in the direction of the trend before finally entering into a long position.

What makes multiple timeframe trading so powerful is that it puts traders on the right side of the market while also pinpointing the highest probability entries available. Perhaps the best manifestation of multiple timeframe trading can be found in Dr. Alexander Elder's Triple Screen, as described in the following Tips & Techniques section.

 TIPS AND TECHNIQUES

The Triple Screen

Dr. Alexander Elder, a psychiatrist by trade and an expert in technical analysis, is one of the world's foremost authorities on trading. Among other prominent books, Elder wrote the international best-selling classic, *Trading for a Living*, and the comprehensive trading tome, *Come Into My Trading Room: A Complete Guide to Trading*.

TIPS AND TECHNIQUES (CONTINUED)

In both of these classics, he writes about one of his most well-known trading strategies based upon the multiple timeframe approach. It is called the "Triple Screen."

In *Come Into My Trading Room: A Complete Guide to Trading* (John Wiley & Sons, 2002), Elder writes,

> "Triple Screen resolves contradictions between indicators and timeframes. It reaches strategic decisions on long-term charts, using trend-following indicators—this is the first screen. It proceeds to make tactical decisions about entries and exits on the intermediate charts, using oscillators—this is the second screen. It offers several methods for placing buy and sell orders—this is the third screen, which we may implement using either intermediate- or short-term charts."

> "Begin by choosing your favorite timeframe, the one with whose charts you like to work, and call it intermediate. Multiply its length by five to find your long-term timeframe. Apply trend-following indicators to long-term charts to reach a strategic decision to go long, short, or stand aside. Standing aside is a legitimate position. If the long-term chart is bullish or bearish, return to the intermediate charts and use oscillators to look for entry and exit points in the direction of the long-term trend. Set stops and profit targets before switching to short-term charts, if available, to fine-tune entries and exits."

Elder's Triple Screen is a simple but ingenious multiple timeframe approach to forex trading. To trade this technique, the trader would begin with a favorite timeframe, like a 4-hour chart, and call it intermediate. To get the long-term chart, the intermediate chart would be multiplied by five (a factor of 4–6 times may actually be more flexible and practical). Therefore, the

> **TIPS AND TECHNIQUES (CONTINUED)**
>
> long-term chart might be the daily chart (4-hour chart × 6 = 24–hour chart). To get the short-term chart, the intermediate chart would be divided by 4-6. Therefore, the short-term chart in this case might be a 1-hour chart (4-hour chart ÷ 4 = 1-hour chart).
>
> On the long-term chart, the first screen, one would focus on trend-following indicators like moving averages, MACD, or trendlines to decide whether to go long, sell short, or stay out of trading altogether due to a lack of trend. On the intermediate chart, the second screen, one would use oscillators like Stochastics or RSI to identify a likely pullback entry zone. Finally, on the short-term chart, the third screen, one would look for a support/resistance breakout in the direction of the long-term trend to pinpoint the trade entry.

Point & Figure Trading—Pointing Out Breakouts

Though visually distinct from all the other chart-trading strategies discussed thus far, point & figure (p&f) trading is, in many ways, very similar to traditional support and resistance breakout trading on bar or candlestick charts. The primary difference lies in the look and functionality of the price charts themselves. Many forex charting platforms include an option to view charts using the p&f structure. As described in Chapter 3, p&f charts actually represent price in a radically different manner from the more familiar bar and candlestick charts. Exhibit 5.15, which displays a typical forex p&f chart, shows just how differently they can look.

Point & figure trading is trading that is based exclusively upon price action, which makes it ideally suited to the foreign exchange market. Originating in the 19th century, this type of financial

EXHIBIT 5.15

Point & Figure Chart

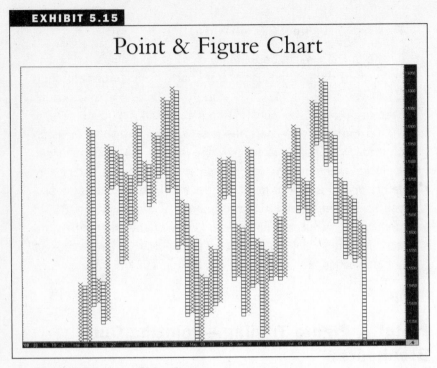

Source: FX Solutions – FX AccuCharts

charting is older than some of the more popular charting methods in common use today. P&f charts are a pure price action play because these charts generally exclude all other elements (like time, volume, and opens/closes) other than price. Therefore, a p&f practitioner can focus all attention on the behavior of price action, which is the most important factor from a technical analysis perspective. Without extraneous elements to clutter the landscape, p&f charts excel at representing clear evidence of such important technical characteristics as trend, support/resistance, and breakouts.

As shown in Exhibit 5.15, p&f charts are constructed with columns of boxes alternately labeled with Xs and Os. An X column means that price has risen in that column. Conversely, an O column means that price has declined in that column. When a reversal occurs on any column, a new column is created going in the opposite direction. As mentioned earlier, there is no time, volume, opens, or closes on p&f charts. Only when price moves a sufficient amount, regardless of time, will an existing column grow or a new column be started.

Two extremely important variables can alter the way p&f charts look and act. The first variable is box size. This is the minimum amount that price needs to move before a new box within an existing column is created. For example, if a column of Xs (which denotes a rising trend) has 10 boxes in the column, price would need to move an additional amount equal to the preset box size before another X would be added onto the top of the column. For example, if a trader sets the box size on the p&f charting software to 10 pips per box, which is a common setting, price would need to move 10 pips above each X box in order to add another X box on top. In the same way, price would need to move 10 pips lower than each box in an O column in order to add another O box on the bottom of the column.

The second important variable is reversal amount. This is the amount of pips that price needs to reverse before a new column is created. A new column is only started when a reversal in an existing column exceeds the reversal threshold. The most common setting for the reversal amount is three boxes, or three "points." If the box size is set at 10 pips and the reversal amount is set at three boxes, the reversal amount in pips is 30 pips. So in a rising column of X boxes, for example, price would need to turn back down against the uptrend by at least 30 pips before a new O column would be started.

The significance of these two variables should be fully recognized and appreciated, as they are what make p&f charts so effective at representing only the most important major market moves, disregarding all of the minor fluctuations known as "noise." For this reason, p&f charts are excellent indicators of both trend and support/resistance.

Because p&f charts outline support and resistance so well, one of the primary trading strategies in most common use with these charts is breakout trading. One notable distinction between bar charting and p&f charting, within the realm of support/resistance, lies in the interpretation of double and triple tops and bottoms. In the world of bar and candlestick charting, a double top is a potentially bearish reversal signal. In p&f terminology, however, a double top is a resistance point where traders should be looking for a bullish break to the upside. The same distinction holds true for double bottoms, as well as triple tops and bottoms.

P&f charts also have their own version of diagonal trendlines, which are drawn at strict 45 degree angles. Chart patterns like triangles are very prevalent as well. Like the horizontal support and resistance levels on these charts, the main method for trading trendlines and patterns on p&f charts is through breakouts.

Because point & figure trading focuses exclusively on price action, the most important aspect of technical trading, p&f practitioners are able to view and interpret market movement with exceptional clarity. Perhaps for this reason, p&f charts have withstood the test of hundreds of years to fulfill one of its current roles today as an increasingly relevant analytical tool for foreign exchange traders.

Carry Trading—In the Interest of Interest

As discussed in Chapter 4 on fundamental analysis, carry trading involves the simultaneous purchase of a high-interest currency and sale of a low-interest currency. This creates an interest rate differential yield that the trader can earn on a daily basis.

The carry trade is primarily a longer-term fundamental investment strategy that seeks to earn this interest rate differential while assuming the substantial risks of exchange rate volatility. A strategy that combines the carry trade with technical analysis to help mitigate this risk will be described in this section's Tips & Techniques.

The fundamental concept behind the carry trade is that when investors' risk aversion is not exceedingly high, international capital tends to flow towards higher-yielding currencies, thereby contributing to a general exchange rate appreciation in these currencies at the expense of the lower-yielding currencies. Of course, this is far from a rule, but only a tendency that occurs when the overall market sentiment is towards a greater risk appetite (as opposed to greater risk aversion).

It should be stressed here that interest rate differentials go both ways, and that if a trade carries a negative interest rate differential, the daily charges to the trader's account on open positions can become prohibitively expensive in many instances. This is because the interest rate differential, whether the trader is paid or charged the amount, is based on the full leveraged size of the trade as opposed to just the fractional amount that the trader puts up in margin for the trade. So, for example, if $1,000 is required to open a full $100,000 position at 100:1 leverage, any interest rate differential on the trade would be paid or charged as a percentage of the full $100,000 amount instead of just the $1,000 amount. This can add up to a substantial sum if a trade is kept open over a prolonged period of time.

At the time of this writing, a commonly carry-traded currency pair is the NZD/JPY, which presently carries a large interest rate differential. The New Zealand dollar currently has a high interest rate while the Japanese yen has a low interest rate. Carry traders who are long NZD/JPY, which means they have borrowed JPY to buy NZD, would be paid based on the high interest rate differential. Conversely, non-carry traders who are short NZD/JPY, which means they have borrowed NZD to buy JPY, would be charged based upon the high interest rate differential.

With most retail foreign exchange brokers, this payment or charge is settled at "rollover," which generally occurs at the end of each business day. This time can vary among brokers. During rollover, open positions that carry a positive interest rate differential are credited directly into the traders' trading accounts. Conversely, those positions that carry a negative interest rate differential are debited directly from the traders' trading accounts.

Carry trading allows foreign exchange traders to receive substantial interest payments on a daily basis for holding high-interest positions open. Of course, the risk of adverse price moves can potentially erase all of those daily interest gains, and then some. But with the help of a high probability carry trading strategy (as described next) and solid risk controls, trading exclusively in the direction of positive interest yield is one of the most prudent and sensible ways to trade long-term positions in forex.

TIPS AND TECHNIQUES

The Technical Carry Trade

A variation on traditional buy-and-hold carry trading incorporates the intelligent use of technical analysis. This method is aptly named, Technical Carry Trading. What sets this approach apart from traditional carry trading is its strict trade entry criteria that screens out low-probability carry trades where price has already over-extended itself. Technical carry trading is a simple strategy for optimizing trade entries/exits that decreases exchange rate risk and maximizes potential exchange rate profit, while also taking advantage of daily interest payments based upon the traditional carry trade model.

The principle behind technical carry trading is that the highest probability strategic entries into long-term carry trade positions are near long-term support/resistance levels. Therefore, if a substantial positive interest rate differential can be achieved by buying (going long) a currency pair (as in the example of NZD/JPY), the highest probability entry would be near long-term support. When price on the pair is near long-term support, the historical probability is that price should eventually rise. On the flip side, if the positive interest differential can be attained by selling short a currency pair, the highest probability entry would be near long-term resistance.

The first step in technical carry trading is to identify those currency pairs that have a high enough interest rate differential to warrant holding a long-term carry position. The threshold might be set at around 300 basis points (or 3 percentage points) or more. Perhaps more importantly, however, the likely future direction of the rate differential should be examined, as this will affect the exchange rate outlook of the currency pair enormously. The future direction of interest rates can be analyzed through central bank statements, economic conditions, the inflation outlook, and other fundamental analyses of the countries/regions in question.

After screening currency pairs according to the current and potential future interest rate differentials, the second step in the technical carry trade process is technical selection. Of the currency pairs chosen in the first step, the trader might choose to trade only those pairs whose current price is in the bottom one-third of their long-term vertical range (near support). Or, if a pair is entrenched in a long-term uptrend channel, the trader may choose only to enter long when price is near the bottom of the channel (again, near support). The primary principle here is to trade only when price is in a high-probability location, like near support when going long or near resistance when selling short.

The last step in the technical carry trade process is trade execution. In order to spread risk and avoid the need to pinpoint entries, technical carry trading may employ a scaled-entry approach. This involves entering into a long-term carry trade using multiple fractional entries. These smaller positions would be spaced evenly within a support/resistance trading zone (as in the bottom one-third of a long-term range) in order to distribute risk across a wide price region. Exits in the form of profit limits and stop losses would be technically based. If a long carry trade is entered near support, the profit target could be placed near resistance (e.g., the top one-third of the long-term range). Stop losses on a long carry trade could be placed somewhere right below long-term support, much like with other types of technical trades.

Technical carry trading is all about increasing the chances of a profitable trade while simultaneously earning substantial leveraged interest. Since good trading, in general, involves maximizing probabilities under precarious circumstances, the technical carry trade strategy performs its function well. At the very least, it improves the outlook of the traditional carry trade dramatically.

News Trading—All the News That's Fit to Profit From

Like carry trading, news trading also falls under the general category of fundamental analysis. News trading is simply the attempt to exploit immediate market reactions to major news and economic data announcements.

Many forex news traders will wait patiently before each major news announcement (as described in Chapter 4), ready to pounce on a trade if the opportunity presents itself. These traders often will have already memorized the consensus (expected) numbers, and would then just wait to see if the actual numbers announced on their up-to-the-second news feed differ considerably from the consensus. If so, the direction of the trade according to the deviation from consensus is determined, and the trade is taken. If all works well on a trade like this, the trader will have jumped on a strong price run either early on or somewhere in the middle of the movement.

Some news traders employ a variation of this method by just watching and waiting during the initial price reaction to the news, which they deem to be unreliable, and then entering the trade on the secondary reaction. This secondary reaction could either be a complete reversal of the initial reaction, or it could be a continuation of the initial move after a pullback or consolidation. This approach is perhaps easier and less frenzied than the first type of news trading, as success in this case does not necessarily depend entirely upon the speed of entry.

Yet other news traders will wait for the news to come out, and then trade technically in the attempts to capture quick profits. Technical trading in this manner necessitates the analysis of very-short-term price charts, pinpointing precise support/resistance levels and momentum signals. This type of ultra-short-term technical analysis presents its own set of issues and difficulties. But when done correctly, it can certainly lend considerably to the news trading process.

Generally, news trading is one of the most challenging and difficult approaches to forex. But if a trader has all of the necessary tools and sensibilities to tackle this type of trading, there are certainly potential profits to be made from the news.

Contrarian Trading—The Majority Doesn't Rule

Unlike most of the other methods and strategies discussed in this chapter, contrarian trading is more of a philosophy than a specific method or strategy. The root of this philosophy lies in the assumption that the general consensus is wrong, and that the astute trader can profitably exploit this by taking the opposite side of the consensus.

Putting this into practice can take several forms. One way to be a contrarian is to pay close attention to what mass media headlines are saying—and then planning trades in the opposite direction. For example, after a prolonged drop in the U.S. dollar's exchange rate, once the mass media begin to foretell a doomsday scenario for the dollar, contrarians may begin looking into either buying the dollar or covering their shorts. Conversely, when mass media portray a rosy picture of the U.S. dollar after a prolonged exchange rate appreciation, a contrarian may soon wish either to go short or close out existing longs.

The simple logic behind this philosophy is the belief that the news media, in reflecting and influencing general public sentiment, are usually either wrong, extremely late, or both. The contrarian assumption is that by the time the mass media have begun to highlight market extremes, there is usually not a great deal more uncommitted capital available to move price much further in the same direction. In other words, if almost everyone has already bought into the euro, and then the media begin saying that the euro should keep going up, who else is left to continue pushing price action much further from there? The amount of new capital that is available to be injected into the currency diminishes dramatically once the major traders have already staked out their positions in the market.

This form of contrarian thinking also comprises the primary idea behind one method of applying the Commodity Futures Trading Commission's (CFTC) Commitments of Traders (COT) Report. Among other valuable pieces of information, this weekly document issued by the CFTC displays slightly delayed reporting on the net positioning of major market players in the currency futures markets. By revealing the net futures positioning of these major players, this COT document can be used by contrarians to trade against extreme relative positioning in the spot forex market.

For example, if the COT report shows that major speculators have been drastically and increasingly net long in the British pound against the U.S. dollar in the past several months, and the current data has just hit the recent peak high in the magnitude of these net long positions, traders may begin looking for the next opportunity to short the pound in a classic contrarian maneuver. Again, the logic here is that if all the large players have already bought the British pound throughout a long and swift price run-up, who else is left to keep pushing price up even further? Therefore, the contrarian indication in this hypothetical COT

EXHIBIT 5.16

COT Report

```
BRITISH POUND STERLING - CHICAGO MERCANTILE EXCHANGE        Code-096742
FUTURES ONLY POSITIONS AS OF 08/26/08                     |
                                                          | NONREPORTABLE
     NON-COMMERCIAL     |    COMMERCIAL    |    TOTAL     | POSITIONS
------------------------|------------------|--------------|---------------
 LONG | SHORT |SPREADS  | LONG  | SHORT    | LONG | SHORT | LONG | SHORT
-----------------------------------------------------------------------
(CONTRACTS OF GBP 62,500)                        OPEN INTEREST:    115,174
COMMITMENTS
 16,211  61,320   1,614  83,264  20,109 101,089  83,043  14,085  32,131

CHANGES FROM 08/19/08 (CHANGE IN OPEN INTEREST:    5,253)
  1,375   2,756    674   6,002   2,010   8,051   5,440  -2,798    -187

PERCENT OF OPEN INTEREST FOR EACH CATEGORY OF TRADERS
   14.1    53.2    1.4    72.3    17.5    87.8    72.1    12.2    27.9

NUMBER OF TRADERS IN EACH CATEGORY (TOTAL TRADERS:     80)
     11      40      8      21      17      37      61


JAPANESE YEN - CHICAGO MERCANTILE EXCHANGE                 Code-097741
FUTURES ONLY POSITIONS AS OF 08/26/08                     |
                                                          | NONREPORTABLE
     NON-COMMERCIAL     |    COMMERCIAL    |    TOTAL     | POSITIONS
------------------------|------------------|--------------|---------------
 LONG | SHORT |SPREADS  | LONG  | SHORT    | LONG | SHORT | LONG | SHORT
-----------------------------------------------------------------------
(CONTRACTS OF JPY 12,500,000)                    OPEN INTEREST:    209,138
COMMITMENTS
 40,103  60,073    568 146,975 124,878 187,646 185,519  21,492  23,619

CHANGES FROM 08/19/08 (CHANGE IN OPEN INTEREST:   -3,844)
   -830  -3,998     29  -1,481   6,416  -2,282   2,447  -1,562  -6,291

PERCENT OF OPEN INTEREST FOR EACH CATEGORY OF TRADERS
   19.2    28.7    0.3    70.3    59.7    89.7    88.7    10.3    11.3

NUMBER OF TRADERS IN EACH CATEGORY (TOTAL TRADERS:     96)
     29      28      4      26      22      58      51


EURO FX - CHICAGO MERCANTILE EXCHANGE                      Code-099741
FUTURES ONLY POSITIONS AS OF 08/26/08                     |
                                                          | NONREPORTABLE
     NON-COMMERCIAL     |    COMMERCIAL    |    TOTAL     | POSITIONS
------------------------|------------------|--------------|---------------
 LONG | SHORT |SPREADS  | LONG  | SHORT    | LONG | SHORT | LONG | SHORT
-----------------------------------------------------------------------
(CONTRACTS OF EUR 125,000)                       OPEN INTEREST:    154,444
COMMITMENTS
 36,026  69,804   3,328  72,360  34,980 111,714 108,112  42,730  46,332

CHANGES FROM 08/19/08 (CHANGE IN OPEN INTEREST:      976)
 -3,932   9,482   -332  17,074   1,191  12,810  10,341 -11,834  -9,365
```

Source: U.S. Commodity Futures Trading Commission (CFTC) at www.cftc.gov.

example is of a potentially bearish impending price move for the pound. Exhibit 5.16 displays a COT report sample from the CFTC. The current report can be found at the following direct link: www .cftc.gov/dea/futures/deacmesf.htm.

Specific methods for using the COT report to trade forex are beyond the scope of this book, but all forex traders should at least be aware that such a report exists and can be of great use in forming contrarian trade opinions.

Another form of contrarianism occurs in technical trading, especially in the context of breakouts. Because many false breakouts occur on foreign exchange charts, astute contrarian traders have learned to "fade the break," or trade in the opposite direction of the breakout. This strategy was discussed earlier in this chapter in the section on breakout trading. It can be an extremely risky way to trade, as it goes directly against the trend and momentum of the market. But if proper risk controls are put into place, it can also be a very effective way to capitalize on the many false and premature breaks of support and resistance.

Generally, contrarian traders will trade against anything that represents popular opinion. When all of the analysts and media are saying one thing, it is almost certain that the contrarians are doing the opposite. The primary goal of any contrarian trader is to buy the market at a bottom or short the market at a top. These traders relish the thought of competing with less experienced traders who are prone to partake in frenzied buying near peaks and frantic selling near troughs.

Although many traders will agree that contrarian trading often makes a lot of sense, to actually become a practicing contrarian takes an iron will, nerves of steel, and great risk management skills. While contrarian traders are frequently correct in their assumptions, trading against the trend and against the masses can often be an endeavor fraught with potentially disastrous pitfalls. It is certainly not a recommended approach for beginners. But even for experienced contrarian traders, much caution must be taken to ensure that one does not inadvertently step into the path of a speeding train.

Backtesting—History Repeats Itself

For any technical trading strategy that has concrete and specific trade entry/exit rules, backtesting that strategy allows the trader to simulate its expected performance using historical price data. With backtesting, traders can actually test how well their strategies would have done if executed in the past.

Many technical trading strategies possess the qualities to be back-tested effectively. Most importantly, they must not have any ambiguity in their rules. One example of a simple strategy that may easily be backtested is as follows: Go long when the 5-period moving average has crossed above the 20-period moving average AND the MACD Histogram has crossed above the zero line AND DMI+ is above DMI−. Sell short when the 5-period moving average has crossed below the 20-period moving average AND the MACD Histogram has crossed below the zero line AND DMI− is above DMI+. Although this simple example has not been tested by this author, it illustrates the characteristics of a strategy that is conducive to backtesting.

Although a backtest may appear to be the perfect method for identifying the most profitable trading strategies, one major caveat should be mentioned here. Using past price data to simulate future results often misleads traders into believing that their backtested performance will always translate into similar results in actual, real-time trading. Many potential factors can and will make hypotheti-cal performance and actual performance differ significantly. Among these factors is the fact that markets change considerably over time. A strategy that may have worked one way for the past five years may work in an entirely different way for the next five years as the market changes and evolves. Often, for example, technical indica-tors that gave profitable signals in the past are subsequently unable to replicate their performance going forward. This phenomenon can be extremely frustrating, but it is an integral aspect of what makes trading such a challenging endeavor. Additionally, in terms of trade execution, trading a strategy in real-time may be much different from the way the strategy is backtested. These differences can potentially skew the results in a significant manner.

Given that past and hypothetical performance may not always be indicative of future results, however, backtesting is still the best available method for evaluating a strategy without actually trading it in a real-time environment. Backtesting a strategy provides enormous benefits to the trader, most important of which is a reasonable expectation of that strategy's potential worth and usefulness.

There are two primary methods of backtesting a trading strategy. The first, and most popular, method is automated backtesting. This requires software that has this capability. A simple Internet search will produce many links to this type of software. Automated backtesting entails using a specialized program into which a trader inputs the specific rules and criteria of the strategy. The software then automatically applies those rules to past price data and tallies the hypothetical profits, losses, and other pertinent information. An entire picture of past performance is created in this way.

A less-practiced method of backtesting is performed manually and visually by the trader. Armed with concrete strategy rules, the trader would scroll back in time on a chart and manually apply the strategy as if it was in a real-time environment. Performance data would then be recorded manually by the trader. Ideally in this type of backtesting, the trader would advance the chart bar-by-bar in order to refrain from seeing price action subsequent to the trade at hand. This eliminates trading in hindsight, which can be detrimental to an objective backtest.

One of the major disadvantages of manual backtesting, when compared with automated backtesting, is the significant potential for human error in executing simulated trades and recording performance results. Furthermore, it takes a great deal of work and discipline to simulate trades manually over a large data set without straying from the strict rules of the strategy. Finally, the normal range of human emotions and biases that often interfere with actual trading can also be a detrimental factor in achieving objective backtest results. That being said, however, manual backtesting can provide the trader with a real "feel" for actually trading a given strategy. This provides valuable trading experience, albeit simulated, that no automated backtest could possibly provide.

Whether performed manually or automatically, backtesting can be one of the most important elements of finding and/or building a solid trading strategy. This vital practice can save traders a great deal of time and money that might otherwise be wasted on trading unprofitable strategies.

Autotrading—Robots for Hire

Closely tied to backtesting is the concept of autotrading. As mentioned in the previous section, automated backtesting utilizes a software trading platform to place hypothetical trades when predetermined trading signals appear on historical price data. The purpose of this is to test the potential viability and profitability of a trading strategy. Autotrading goes a step further by actually executing real trades on current, real-time market prices. When a predetermined signal emerges, the software actually places a trade automatically.

This is usually initiated only when all proper backtesting has indicated the likely success of the trading system.

Autotrading is common in foreign exchange trading. Many hedge funds and other entities that manage money via forex trading use some form of autotrading in their daily activities. In addition, many private, individual traders have also begun to adopt autotrading to execute their thoroughly backtested and highly optimized forex trading strategies.

For these traders, autotrading is accomplished using an Application Programming Interface (API), which connects the trader's system to the dealer's trade execution structure. APIs require programming skills on the part of either the trader or a programmer hired by the trader. But once all of the trading rules and criteria are determined by the trader, programming an API can be relatively straightforward for anyone with programming experience.

After the specific trading rules and criteria are determined, the strategy is backtested with positive results, and the API is programmed, autotrading is almost as simple as flipping a switch to begin the trading process. When this occurs, not only are trades entered when predetermined technical criteria are met, but trade exits in the form of stop losses and profit limits can also be programmed into the API. This creates an entire self-contained system for trading foreign exchange.

As with backtesting, any nondiscretionary technical trading strategy that has clear-cut, unambiguous rules is a good candidate for autotrading. In fact, if a trader has optimized and perfected this type of a black-and-white trading strategy that runs devoid of human judgment, autotrading is perhaps the best way to execute it, as it effectively eliminates all human biases, errors, and emotions in the trading process.

Chapter Summary

Three general approaches to forex, including position trading, swing trading, and day trading, outline the primary styles that have been adopted by many forex traders in the market today. Position trading attempts to capitalize on longer-term trends, and can employ both fundamental and technical analysis to determine directional bias. Swing trading is generally a purely technical style that looks to exploit short- to medium-term swings, or turns, in the market. Day trading is the shortest-term approach that seeks to get in and out of position within a given trading day using extremely short charting timeframes and well-defined technical signals.

Besides these general approaches to trading foreign exchange, there are other delineations of trading methodology. On the technical trading side, these include trend trading, range trading, breakout trading, and pattern trading. Trend trading, or trend following, utilizes primarily technical analysis to identify the overall trend, and then to determine the best place to enter that trend. In the absence of a trend, traders will often go into range trading mode, where lows are bought and highs are sold during sideways trading ranges. When a range or support/resistance level is broken to the upside or to the downside, breakout trading takes precedence. Traders will then buy on a break above or sell on a break below. One type of breakout trading occurs when chart patterns are broken. Common examples of traded patterns include head-and-shoulders, triangles, wedges, flags, and pennants.

Yet other common methods for trading forex include strategies that utilize the powerful analytical tools of Fibonacci, pivot points, and Elliott Wave. Each of these tools commands its own loyal following among traders, and each has its own unique approach to forecasting price movement.

Divergence trading seeks to identify instances when price and an oscillator are diverging in direction. This often means a potential loss of momentum in the prevailing price direction and therefore a possible impending reversal. Divergence signals are often reliable in helping to forecast or confirm these potential market turns.

Multiple timeframe trading is an excellent all-encompassing methodology for entering into high-probability currency trades. Starting on the longest timeframes to identify trend, multiple timeframe traders then drill down to progressively shorter timeframes in order to determine, and ultimately pinpoint, the most advantageous trade entry points.

Point & figure trading utilizes an entirely different type of chart from the commonly used bar or candlestick charts. Point & figure charts are filled with Xs and Os, and they excel at identifying trends, support/resistance, and breakouts, while minimizing the representation of market noise.

On the fundamental analysis side, carry trading, news trading, and contrarian trading are some of the primary strategies and methods. Carry trading works on the interest rate differential inherent in currency pairs, and seeks to earn a positive yield on both this differential and directional exchange rate movement. News trading exploits price spikes and other types of fast price action that occur around economic data releases and fundamental news announcements. Contrarian trading takes the position that the general consensus as expressed by the media, the analysts, and the trading public, is inherently wrong, and that it is best to trade against this consensus at market extremes.

Finally, backtesting and autotrading are two important components of implementing trading strategies that generally do not rely upon the trader's judgments or discretion. These types of strategies are primarily technical in nature, and they must necessarily have rules and criteria that are unambiguous. Backtesting allows the trader to determine if a given strategy would have been profitable using past price data, which is an indication of how it might potentially perform in the future. In contrast, autotrading actually executes real trades automatically according to a pre-programmed set of instructions that sets trade entries, stop losses, and profit limits.

CHAPTER 6

Important Elements of Successful Foreign Exchange Trading

After reading this chapter, you will be able to:

- Understand some of the most important elements of successful trading that many novice traders are reluctant to learn.

- Recognize the crucial difference that good risk management and money management can make in forex trading.

- Realize that most experienced and successful traders hold the preservation of capital as their top priority, thereby helping to ensure that they are at least around to trade another day.

- Apply proper and consistent trading discipline to strive for the best chances of success in forex trading

- Appreciate the necessary elements that go into a comprehensive trading plan.

The Boring Side of Success

After all of the excitement learning about trading strategies that seem to hold great promise of future profits, most novice traders are reluctant to come back down to earth and learn about the "boring" side of successful trading. This includes risk management and money management, discipline and psychology, and a proper trading plan.

Some novice traders may deem these subjects unnecessary, as long as their "sure-thing" trading strategy produces profits. But this line of thinking could not be further from the truth. In order to maintain any hope of becoming consistently successful, traders must learn and internalize certain good habits that have nothing to do with market analysis or the mechanics of putting in trades. Rather, these crucial elements of intelligent trading constitute a way of life that virtually all of the most successful traders have adopted to one degree or another. Let us begin with a discussion of risk.

A Risky Business

Perhaps more than any other type of financial trading, foreign exchange trading makes it extremely difficult for inexperienced traders to manage risk effectively. This is partly due to the fact that the leverage offered in forex is so high when compared with other markets. When $1 in margin can control $100 or more in a trade, the potential for profit is magnified to an extreme degree. But many beginners seem to forget that the risk of ruin is magnified just as much. High leverage can certainly be a powerful feature in a positive way, but it can also have a way of tempting unsuspecting traders into becoming reckless and greedy. As we will soon find out, recklessness and greed are two characteristics that, at some point, will invariably destroy a trading account.

This brings us to the number one priority of successful traders—preservation of capital. Risk and money must be managed in a way that the ultimate goal is to survive to trade another day. Without this, all is lost and the game is over. Many experienced traders go a step further by subscribing to the winning philosophy that if virtually every ounce of focus is concentrated on preserving capital, the profits will take care of themselves.

Fatter Is Healthier (But Only for Trading Accounts)

There are many important ways in which traders can work toward the goal of preserving capital. The most obvious initial step is to have enough capital to begin with. But how much is "enough?" First, it depends on the amount of risk capital one can afford to put aside for trading without substantially impacting one's lifestyle. Then, it depends on the size of the positions that one will be trading. But just because there is sufficient margin on account to open a certain position, does not mean that a trader has sufficient capital to trade successfully. For example, many beginners believe that if $1000 is required as margin for one standard lot trade of $100,000 at 100:1 leverage, $1000 is enough capital to have in the account for making the trade. This could not be further from the truth. Having only enough funds in an account to cover the minimum required margin for a given position is one of the quickest routes to disaster.

The exact amount of money that is considered "enough" and sufficiently capitalized will vary from trader to trader. But one general guideline used by many prudent retail traders is always to have in the account, at the very least, ten times the amount of margin required for a typical trade. So, for example, if a trader wishes to trade one mini-lot of $10,000 at a time at 100:1 leverage, where the margin required is $100, that trader should always have at least $1000 in the account. By the same token, if a trader wishes to trade one standard lot of $100,000 at a time at 100:1 leverage, where the margin required is $1000, that trader should always have $10,000 in the account at the very least. This, again, is only a very general guideline, as each trader's risk profile and risk appetite will necessarily differ.

Risk and Reward

After overcoming the first hurdle of being properly capitalized, the trader can then turn attention to creating a risk/money management plan to preserve capital. One of the key components of this plan is to set consistent risk parameters with regard to stop losses and profit targets. These should be set in accordance with a properly planned risk:reward, or perhaps more aptly named, "reward-to-risk" ratio.

The reward-to-risk ratio is a simple concept that can work wonders for the overall profitability of an account. While optimal reward-to-risk ratios can be difficult to attain in everyday trading, foreign exchange traders should always strive for the best, or highest, ratios possible. A rather high ratio like 4:1, for example, simply means that on any given trade, a trader is looking to profit by four times the amount that the trader is prepared to lose. In real-world terms, this means that if a trade is entered with a 30 pip stop loss, for example, the profit target would be set at least at 120 pips. The ramifications of the reward-to-risk ratio are considerable. With a good ratio, traders can actually lose significantly more trades than they win, and still be consistently profitable. This is because their average profits are much larger than their average losses. The concept of a high reward-to-risk ratio lends itself well to the oft-repeated trader's maxim, "Let your profits run and cut your losses short."

So what exactly is the optimal ratio? It can be difficult in trading foreign exchange to achieve ratios as high as 4:1, because at a certain point with these higher ratios, the trade-off is that losses become much more frequent than wins. Since the wins would be much larger in dollar value than the losses, this is perfectly fine from a long-term profitability standpoint, as mentioned earlier. But the psychological toll of excessively frequent losses, even if relatively small in value, can eventually become devastating to a trader's psyche. Generally speaking, many forex traders like to target a reward-to-risk ratio of 3:1 as the ideal. This means that each profit is targeted to be at least three times as large as each loss.

While 3:1 may be optimal, however, shooting for 2:1 can often be more practical in many real-life trading situations. The trick in consistently achieving good ratios like these lies in adapting the ratios to prevailing market conditions. For example, if a certain chart pattern is identified on a currency pair, the technical trader will need to make sure that a profit target two or three times the magnitude of the stop loss is realistic before taking the trade. This is just prudent trading. But if the trader rigidly adheres to unrealistically high ratio requirements, this may result in too many voluntarily missed opportunities. The best solution is often the middle path—a reward-to-risk ratio that is high enough to achieve long-term profitability, while low enough to fit market conditions realistically. Therefore, the true optimal ratio ultimately depends on each trader's own experimentation and what works best through actual experience.

Fix Your Fractions

Besides finding the right reward-to-risk balance, another important aspect of a money management plan that focuses on capital preservation is called fixed fractional money management. This generally refers to the percentage of total account equity that a trader is willing to risk on each trade. So, for example, if a trading account has $1000 in it, and the trader trades one mini-lot (10,000 units) at a time for approximately $1 per pip, a fixed fractional plan of 3% of total equity would necessitate a 30-pip maximum stop loss on each mini-lot trade. Why? Because if the trader wants the maximum risk per trade to be set at 3% of $1000, or $30, and each pip is worth about $1, that would mean the trader could accept losing up to 30 pips on each trade. This would necessitate putting in stop losses that are a maximum of 30 pips away from the trade entry for all trades.

Contrary to the common belief that fixed fractional money management refers directly to the percentage of account equity actually put up to make a trade, the real meaning generally refers to the percentage of total funds placed at risk on each trade as it relates to stop loss placement (along with position sizing). Therefore, the fact that $100 of a trading account's total $1000 is put up in margin for a trade does not necessarily mean that 10% of account equity is being risked on this trade. Only if a stop loss of 100 pips (at a value of $1 per pip) is instituted into this trade would 10% of total equity actually be risked.

Many traders do not favor fixed fractional money management because it encourages the basing of stop losses on an arbitrary number that generally has very little to do with prevailing market and trading conditions. For example, a 30-pip stop loss may be perfectly reasonable for a trendline breakout trade on an hourly chart, but may be completely inappropriate for a head-and-shoulders trade on a weekly chart. Just because the fixed fractional percentage may work well for a trader's money management profile, does not make it appropriate for every type of trade entered.

At the same time, however, fixed fractional money management, when used more as a restraining guideline than as a strict stop loss value, can serve as a very effective deterrent against the self-destruction of a trading account. So instead of specifying an exact (fixed) percentage risk for each trade, it often works better for traders to loosen the percentage and make it a maximum risk parameter. For instance, instead of creating the rigid rule that exactly 2% of total equity will be risked on each trade, a more adaptable rule might be to require that no single trade can have a stop loss that exceeds, for example, 4% of total equity. As long as the stop loss represents less than the predetermined maximum percentage of account equity, it can be fine-tuned, with the additional help of position-sizing, to suit the prevailing market and trading conditions.

Trailing Stops—Loyal Followers

In general, stop losses are an integral component of good risk management. To go a step further in the right direction, the liberal use of a trailing stop loss strategy can do even more for a trader's bottom line. A trailing stop, as explained in Chapter 2, is a dynamic order to close a trade at progressively better prices.

So, for example, a trader buys EUR/USD and applies a 30-pip trailing stop to the trade. If price moves in the profitable direction for this trade (i.e., up), the stop loss follows price by 30 pips. If price moves at least 30 pips above the entry point of the trade, profits begin to be effectively locked in. This process is automatically accomplished by the trailing stop mechanism. If, at anytime, price moves down by 30 pips, the trade gets closed out by the moving stop loss. Theoretically, if there is no profit target set and price keeps moving up forever without fluctuating down by at least 30 pips, the trade could gain unlimited profit. Of course, this would never happen in the real world of trading, but it just displays the potential power of the trailing stop.

From a risk management perspective, trailing stops can automate the twin concepts of cutting losses and letting profits run. A trailing stop ensures that a protective stop loss is always in place, and provides an easy way to secure hard-earned profits on an ongoing basis. Trailing stops can be instituted automatically using a trading platform's trailing stop function, or can be performed manually simply by moving the static stop loss on an open position in logical increments as price moves in the trade's favor.

Size Matters

Very closely related to sufficient capitalization, reward-to-risk ratios, and fixed fractional money management through stop-loss placement, is the sizing of trade positions. Position-sizing is a vital aspect of good money management. In fact, sufficient capital and sensible position-sizing go hand in hand to help curtail risk and prevent the depletion of a trading account.

As discussed earlier in this book, there are three primary position sizes in retail foreign exchange trading. Trading accounts with the smallest equity usually trade the micro, or super-mini, lot. These consist of 1000 units of a given currency, and the dollar value per pip is approximately $0.10. The next size up, traded by slightly larger trading accounts, is called the mini-lot. Mini-lots consist of 10,000 units of a given currency, and the dollar value per pip is approximately $1.00. Finally, for even larger accounts there is the standard lot, which consists of 100,000 units of a given currency and whose per-pip dollar value is approximately $10.00. Trading accounts that are even larger than this may trade in multiple standard lots at a time.

Which size is best? It all depends on how well capitalized the account is, as well as the particular risk profile of the trader. As noted earlier in this chapter within the section on being properly capitalized, there are some rough guidelines that many prudent traders follow when planning their trade size and account capitalization. For example, a trader planning on trading standard lots of $100,000, where the margin required per trade is $1000 (at 100:1 leverage), would probably want to have $10,000 in trading account equity, at the very least. At the same time, however, this does not necessarily mean that a trader with $10,000 in a trading account has to trade in standard lots. Mini-lots are perfectly fine, even for larger accounts, and they actually have an advantage over standard lots. Mini-lots are much more flexible than standard lots in providing the ability to trade in odd unit sizes (e.g., 70,000 currency units traded with 7 mini-lots, as opposed to a 100,000 unit minimum for standard lots). In addition, mini-lots can accommodate multiple fractional positions (as explained later in this section).

Clearly, one of the most significant results of trading larger lot sizes is the increased dollar value per pip. Among other effects of higher pip value is that it can obviously impact trading psychology a great deal. Any trader knows the difference between having a small amount on the line and having a great deal on the line. A trader watching $1/pip price movements is generally less apt to sweat and make rash trading decisions than the one watching $10/pip price movements.

Overtrading with regard to position-sizing often forces the trader either to abandon proper money management principles or set stop losses that are unrealistically close. This is due to the fact that in order to retain the same risk profile, higher pip values necessarily mean a smaller number of pips to cushion the trade. The primary point about proper position-sizing is to avoid overextending account capital and getting into financially uncomfortable trading situations.

Closely related to overall position-sizing in the realm of risk management is the concept of multiple fractional positions. This is yet another method to help spread and control risk. Multiple fractional positions are smaller components of the main trade. These smaller positions may be entered all at the same time, and then each fractional position can progressively be closed in a staggered manner to lock in profits as the position moves in a profitable direction. So, for example, if a trader enters into a long position using 10 mini-lots (instead of 1 standard lot), each mini-lot can be closed for a profit as the price increases, thereby securing partial profits in a progressive fashion.

Another method of spreading risk using multiple fractional positions employs staggered entries, as opposed to staggered exits. Each fractional position would be entered at a different price level. Because it is extremely difficult to pinpoint precisely the best single entry on a trade, multiple fractional entries allow traders to get in on a position within a flexible price range instead of at just one price, thereby spreading some risk among different price levels.

Position Overload

Also closely related to overall position-sizing is the common afflic-tion of overtrading by opening too many full-sized positions (as opposed to fractional) at the same time. In foreign exchange trading, the danger in overtrading lies in more than just the overextension of account margin, although that is also of grave concern.

The danger that is often overlooked in this market stems from the fact that, relatively speaking, there are so few different instru-ments that are practically tradable. This means that it is extremely difficult, if not virtually impossible, to diversify holdings adequately. In addition, the primary trading instruments in foreign exchange trading are correlated very closely with one another. This can be either a positive correlation or a negative correlation.

In the world of equities trading, finding diverse, noncorrelated investments can be relatively straightforward. In forex, on the other hand, the four most actively traded currency pairs, EUR/USD, USD/JPY, GBP/USD, and USD/CHF, are all dependent on the relative value of the U.S. dollar. The same is true for the next most actively traded pairs, AUD/USD and USD/CAD. Beyond this, there are only a handful of common cross currency pairs that are not dollar-based, like EUR/GBP, EUR/JPY, GBP/JPY, and so on, but these are also extremely interrelated. Rounding out the list, most of the exotic pairs are not even practically tradable because of their intolerably wide spreads stemming from their low liquidity. So if a trader/investor is involved solely in the forex market, diversification is simply not a viable option.

Therefore, overtrading in forex can be doubly dangerous. Not only does it create risk in overextending margin, but it also increases exposure to highly correlated instruments.

There are several ways to help mitigate this type of risk. The most obvious way is to place a strict maximum on the number of positions entered at one time. This means that the trader must simply have the discipline to refrain from overtrading. Another way is to reduce the size of each individual trade, as in multiple fractional positions. This is an easier method, as it allows the trader to enter the same number of positions as usual, while committing a much smaller amount to each position.

Yet another method for combating correlation risk that many novice traders try in the beginning of their forex explorations centers around attempting to structure a hedged currency portfolio for controlling risk. For example, since EUR/USD and USD/CHF generally have a relatively high negative correlation, going long in both or going short in both could potentially be considered akin to a hedged position with significantly reduced risk.

In actuality, however, there is really no reason to trade like this, even if it does succeed in controlling volatility risk to a substantial degree. Because currencies are traded in pairs, going long in correlated pairs like EUR/USD and USD/CHF, for example, simply creates a synthetic pairing that is akin to just going long a third pair, in this case EUR/CHF. In the same way, being short both EUR/USD and USD/CHF is like being short just EUR/CHF. The risk reduction in quasi-hedging of this nature is limited to reducing exposure to volatility by trading the much tamer EUR/CHF pair as opposed to the much more volatile EUR/USD or USD/CHF pair. Therefore, the entire exercise of opening two opposing positions does not make a great deal of sense, as the same goal can be accomplished by the much simpler act of trading just the one synthetic pair.

Other traders utilize their broker's hedging functionality, which gives the ability to be long and short in the same currency pair at the same time, in the hopes that it will provide a reduced risk environment for trading. The issue with this perspective, however, is that without any risk exposure to the market, neither profits nor losses can be made. So it is akin to not having any position at all. Therefore, hedging within the forex market, though it may be a component of certain specialized trading strategies, is not one of the more viable methods for controlling risk in general forex trading.

In short, there are really no shortcuts to proper risk and money management. The best ways to combat the tendency to overtrade is simply either to cut back on the number of positions opened or reduce the size of each position.

Measuring Risk with a Trendline

As touched upon earlier in the book, the primary analytical method for measuring and controlling risk from a trading strategy perspective lies in the use of technical analysis. One of the greatest strengths of technical analysis is that it allows traders to quantify precisely, and thereby help control, the risk factors inherent in trading.

The most obvious risk control application of technical analysis is stop-loss placement. Technical analysis employs a simple and elegant rationale for determining the location of stop losses. When the technical reasons for getting into a trading position no longer exist or are no longer valid, that position should be abandoned, even if at a loss. The purpose of a stop loss, after all, is to cut losses while those losses are still manageable.

For example, in a potential breakout situation where a trade is entered on a breakout above a certain price level, if price subsequently falls back below that level, the reasons for entering the trade are no longer valid. Therefore, the stop loss should be placed right underneath the breakout level, where the break will have proven itself to be either false or premature. A failed breakout, as described above, is certainly a good reason to get out of a trade with a manageable loss.

Here is another example of risk management from a technical analysis perspective. For a trader who has entered a short position on a pullback up to a downtrend resistance line, if on one of the subsequent pullbacks price exceeds that downtrend line by a significant amount, a good location for a stop loss would be right above the trendline. A break above the descending trendline would mean that price is no longer pulling back and continuing the downtrend, but might perhaps be reversing its trend. If this is the case, a properly

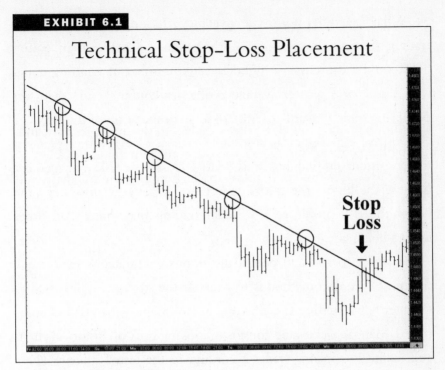

EXHIBIT 6.1

Technical Stop-Loss Placement

Stop
Loss

Source: FX Solutions – FX AccuCharts

placed stop loss above the line can potentially prevent a great deal of pain. See Exhibit 6.1.

Technical analysis, therefore, can be an essential component of an effective risk management plan.

Great Expectations

Another way in which risk management is related to trading strategy lies in the concept of positive expectancy. Even with all of the best money management practices and risk control methods in the world, a trader should not hope to achieve consistent profitability without a trading strategy that delivers a positive expectancy.

What exactly is positive expectancy? It simply means that the trading strategy should consistently produce a net gain in equity. This could mean either a higher average number of winning trades than losses, or a greater average profit per winning trade than loss per losing trade (reward-to-risk), or any combination of the two.

Positive expectancy is absolutely crucial to every trader's quest for consistent profitability. It is related closely to risk management because the higher the tested expectancy for any given strategy, the better the risk profile of any trader trading that strategy, all other factors being equal.

In order to test and potentially improve a strategy's expectancy, the most common method is to backtest the strategy. As discussed in Chapter 5, backtesting can take one of two forms—manual and automated. Manual backtesting consists of looking back on historical charts and manually applying trades according to the tested strategy. These hypothetical trades should then be observed and recorded to obtain a long-term record of performance. Automated backtesting, on the other hand, employs sophisticated software to apply and record trades automatically on historical price data. Results are quickly delivered to the backtester, and the trader can then try to tweak the parameters of the strategy in order to fine-tune a strategy with a higher expectancy. At least some form of backtesting is extremely helpful, and almost a necessity, for creating a money management plan that works.

Psychologically Speaking

While this entire chapter thus far has been focused on risk and money management, which are extremely vital to a successful trader's skill set, another important aspect of success in forex is trading psychology. Foremost within this realm of trading psychology is the concept of discipline. Greed and fear are the two most dangerous emotions to a trader. Discipline is the remedy for these destructive emotions.

The concept of discipline can take many forms. This includes discipline to:

- Refrain from overtrading
- Adhere to a sensible money management regimen
- Act according to a structured trading plan
- Cut losses and let profits run
- Follow religiously a trading system with a proven positive expectancy
- Trade without succumbing to the destructive emotions of greed and fear
- Avoid chasing a runaway market
- Use stop losses and/or trailing stops
- Stay out of a trade if there is no valid reason to be in that trade

Trading emotionally is one of the easiest ways to be unprofitable in forex. Of course, as humans we could never be devoid of emotion, nor would we ever want to be. But as traders, it is most certainly in our best interests to use discipline to overpower many of the negative effects of emotional trading.

There are many examples of emotional trading that both novice traders and experienced traders alike succumb to on frequent occasions. For one, many traders fall into the trap of trading aggressively, or even angrily, after either a string of losses or one particularly devastating loss. This is often caused by a desire to get back at the market with a vengeance. The trader's underlying sentiment is that the market is the adversary, and that aggressive trading can somehow make back the lost equity, teaching the market a lesson in the process. Clearly, this is irrational behavior that invariably leads to even further devastation of the trading account. Discipline to accept losses gracefully and to continue adhering to the trading plan is the primary weapon against falling into this kind of a psychological trap.

A related trap that is found often in foreign exchange trading occurs when traders experience a winning streak and begin believing that they have mastered the market. Oftentimes, these traders will start thinking that they are unstoppable and that the principles of prudent trading somehow do not apply to them. Greed and recklessness then enter the picture. When this occurs, prior winnings generally turn into subsequent losses, and these traders then become compelled to play catch-up by attempting to make back the winnings. This results in a vicious cycle that eats away quickly at any account, if trading discipline is not reintroduced before it becomes too late.

Another example of emotional trading occurs when traders are alerted to a runaway price move after a large portion of the move has already occurred. The emotion that surfaces is one of fear—fear of missing out on the trade of the decade. Traders in this position that have not mastered the discipline to refrain from acting upon reckless emotions, will often jump into the trade blindly in an attempt to chase the market. They do this even if the entry turns out to be at the worst possible time, like buying at a top, where price has already exhausted itself after a significant upmove. Trading in this manner, without discipline, is a sure method of racking up frequent and substantial losses.

Yet other traders who need to work on developing discipline enter into positions for no other reason than the excitement of trading. To these individuals, trading represents a recreational activity much like gambling or sports, where constant action is the name of the game. When these types of traders treat forex trading as gambling, it can actually become very similar to gambling. If positions are opened purely for the purpose of creating excitement and avoiding boredom, forex can have even worse odds than many casino games. Of course, this is the extreme. The vast majority of forex traders do not constantly act on an insatiable itch for action. For some traders, however, there is usually an occasional need to trade for no other reason than the thrill of it. This type of trading should be avoided at all costs, as it is thoroughly detrimental to a healthy account balance.

It is also detrimental to trading accounts when traders fail to follow their own tested trading methods because of a combination of impatience, greed, fear, and/or other psychological factors. For example, a trader may have backtested a technical trading system that was shown to have a high positive expectancy under diverse market conditions. But suppose this system dictates that three different prerequisites should occur on the chart all at the same time before a trade may be initiated. What will often happen, for a variety of reasons, is that the trader will become anxious to trade, and will therefore start becoming both lazy and lenient on the prerequisites. If the conditions are close enough, the trader may just take the trade. This type of undisciplined trading completely invalidates any backtesting work performed prior to live trading. Therefore, failing to follow a tested strategy faithfully is virtually the same as gambling on an untested strategy.

Finally, to close out this section on discipline and trading psychology, here are just a few words on hoping and wishing. To put it succinctly, there is no room in profitable trading for these two sentiments. The markets will move where they need to move, and no amount of hoping or wishing can change that. No individual forex trader could ever actually will the market to move a certain way. But all day and every day, traders are still trying. Doing so, however, can seriously hurt these traders. When they hope and pray for the best under deteriorating circumstances, they often fail to prepare for the worst. Among other negative consequences, this can mean a failure to cut losses when those losses most need to be cut. The best way to prevent the potentially destructive sentiments of hoping and wishing is to have a strict trading plan and to develop the discipline to follow it consistently, no matter what may happen. This brings us to the next and final section of this chapter and this book.

Plan the Trade and Trade the Plan

The master trading plan should encompass elements of everything that has been discussed throughout this book. This includes a basic foundation in the mechanics of foreign exchange trading, an analytical base including both technical and fundamental analysis, a repertoire of solid trading strategies and methods, a comprehensive risk/money management plan, and a disciplined approach to trading. Every detail of the trading plan should be recorded in a dedicated journal, addressing all aspects of day-to-day trading in order to cover as many contingencies as possible.

At the very least, a solid trading plan should include the following specific elements:

- Amount of starting capital to be used for trading
- Primary lot size and leverage used
- Maximum percentage of trading capital risked on each trade
- Reward-to-risk ratio target
- Realistic daily, weekly, and monthly profit goals
- Specific daily, weekly, and monthly loss limits (the point of monetary loss at which a trader stops trading for the given period)
- An entire description of the trading strategy(s) used
- Specific trade entry criteria according to the tested trading strategy
- Specific trade exit criteria (stop losses, profit limits, and/or manual exits) according to the tested trading strategy

It cannot be emphasized enough how important a good trading plan is to a successful trader. Running a successful business, which is how forex trading should be approached, usually demands some kind of a written business plan at some point. Of course, a business can certainly run without a written business plan, but its potential for success is increased a great deal if there is a plan in place that stresses the vision, direction, and step-by-step process for reaching consistent profitability. Trading is no different.

Besides maintaining this written trading plan, successful traders also take notes every day, recording the trading activities of the day. In this way, these traders can find out if their actions conformed to the plan, and how they can constantly improve their trading habits.

With these good trading habits, along with knowledge, practice, and a well-thought-out trading plan, any individual can hold the blueprint for success in foreign exchange trading. Possessing all of the characteristics of a successful forex trader is not an easy goal. But in the end, it is well worth the effort to get there.

Chapter Summary

Initially, most traders tend to gravitate toward the most tangible aspects of foreign exchange trading that are the easiest to grasp. This includes technical and fundamental analysis, as well as concrete trading methods and strategies. What many of these traders tend to overlook are some of the most important attributes necessary for successful foreign exchange trading.

To begin with, successful traders have learned how to manage risk. This is especially crucial in the highly leveraged world of foreign exchange trading. In order to manage this risk, experienced traders make their highest priority the preservation of capital. In many respects, this can be considered even more important than a focus on just making profits.

A concentration on risk control and the preservation of capital starts with good money management. The most basic requirement for good money management is sufficient capitalization. The amount of capital required depends first on the amount of risk capital one can afford without substantially impacting one's lifestyle. Then, it depends on the planned magnitude of trading and level of risk appetite.

After the capital requirement basics are satisfied, a trader can then turn attention toward reward-to-risk ratios, fixed fractional money management, and potential trailing stop-loss strategies. These all have to do with the proper placement of stop losses in relation to the larger goals of preserving capital, reducing risk, and achieving consistent net profitability.

Beyond these key components of intelligent trading, the trader must additionally address the prudent sizing of trades, which, in turn, also means an avoidance of overloading on positions. Overtrading in this respect carries the danger not only of margin overextension, but also potentially precarious exposure to a nondiversified, highly correlated portfolio of currency holdings.

With regard to the analytical side of trading, technical analysis excels as a method for quantifying and controlling risk through stop loss placement. In addition, any trading strategy employed must ultimately have a significant positive expectancy in order to contribute to a viable money management system and potential net profitability. The expectancy of a strategy can be determined through backtesting, whether manual or automated, where the strategy is applied to past price data in order to evaluate its hypothetical historical performance.

Risk and money cannot be managed effectively without one key component of healthy trading psychology. That component is discipline. Even if all other factors are in place to foster success in foreign exchange trading, a trader will fail without discipline. There are many types of discipline that are essential to achieving consistent profitability in trading, all of which need time and effort to develop. Perhaps the most important discipline is that of adhering to a well-prepared trading plan.

The trading plan brings all the necessary elements of trading into one cohesive whole. It acts as the blueprint and the business plan for traders that are serious about seeking sustainable success in the foreign exchange markets. Perhaps no other tool, whether a chart or a news feed or a crystal ball, carries as significant an impact on a trader's potential success as a good, specific trading plan. It is truly one of the essentials of foreign exchange trading.

Index

Index

Index